The Nation's Top Programs

EXCELLENCE IN LIBRARY SERVICES TO YOUNG ADULTS

Mary K. Chelton, Editor

American Library
Association
► President's Committee ◄
for Customer Service
to Youth

AMERICAN LIBRARY ASSOCIATION
CHICAGO AND LONDON, 1994

Cover design by Richmond Jones

Composition by ALA Production Services, in Linotype Melior and True Type Futuri Extra Condensed using Corel Ventura Publisher and camera-ready pages output on a Varityper VT600 laser printer.

Printed on 50-pound Thor Offset, a pH-neutral stock, and bound in 10-point C1S cover stock by Malloy Lithographing, Inc.

The paper used in this publication meets the minimum requirements of American National Standard for Information Sciences—Permanence of Paper for Printed Library Materials, ANSI Z39.48-1984. ∞

Library of Congress Cataloging-in-Publication Data

Excellence in library services to young adults : the nation's top
    programs / edited by Mary K. Chelton.
            p.   cm.
        Includes bibliographical references and index.
        ISBN 0-8389-3440-4
        1. Public libraries—Services to teenagers—United States—Case
    studies. 2. High school libraries—United States—Case studies.
    I. Chelton, Mary K. II. American Library Association President's
    Committee for Customer Service to Youth.
    Z718.5.E93 1994
    027.62′6′0973—dc20   94-15407

Printed in the United States of America.

98 97 96 95 94   5 4 3 2 1

Contents

Programs and Services

Reading Promotion

Special Needs Populations

Youth Participation

Foreword

Hardy Franklin
April 1939—Rome, Georgia

It was a hot spring day, the kind of day in northwest Georgia that hints at the heat of the summer to come. Hardy was passing the public library on his way to his after school job and realized that he might go in to pick up some books to read to his young charge.

He had often visited the public library with the white family that he helped. The Abercrombies had a little boy that Hardy played with after school, in addition to doing errands and helping around the house. One of the ways they passed time was to read. Hardy would read to Stanley and often they would go with Mrs. Abercrombie to the public library to pick out books.

He stepped into the coolness of the library and walked to the bookshelves where he often found reading he liked. There was a hush, the silence that comes when you know the people in the room are taking in the sequence of events. The silence was sustained until all of a sudden the librarian appeared at his side. "I know that you come here with a family but you can't come in here by yourself," she told Hardy.

Hardy left quickly, emerging into the bright sun and walked down the street quickly to his father's barbershop. His father joined him outside and they walked five blocks toward home and turned around and walked the five blocks back to the barbershop. During the walk his father attempted to soothe him by explaining the "separate but equal" practices prevalent at the time.

Carol Streib
April 1964—Ithaca, New York

She was fifteen years old when her mother suggested she go to the public library and see if there might be a job for her as a page during the summer. Her mother had heard of other children who had jobs at the library.

Carol used the library heavily and most of the library staff knew her, even in a town of over 30,000 people. She presented herself to the woman at the circulation desk and told her she wanted to apply to be a page. The librarian, in a cool tone, asked, "What experience do you have?"

She gulped and asked if that meant experience working at the library or experience working? "The library—library experience," was the reply. Carol told her she didn't have any but she had been a junior camp counselor, had worked as a babysitter, and was a good worker and also familiar with the library.

"Sorry, you have to have library experience," said the librarian.

*November 1991—Haven Middle School
Evanston, Illinois*

The parents were gathered at a curriculum meeting for the seventh grade. The major project of the year, the United Nations report, was described and explained. Each student chose a country and researched the country all year-long, filling a notebook with essays on a variety of assigned topics about their chosen country.

Several parents asked how their kids could get enough information to carry out this large and complex assignment. The response was they could use the library. Several parents noted that the classes did not go to the library on a regular basis, nor was the library open after school. The staff at the middle school mentioned that the library could be open if the student brought a note from his or her parents giving permission to stay after school.

Another parent noted that it was difficult to find information on some of the countries that the students had chosen. The staff responded that the students should have researched what was available and made a better choice.

Peter Nielsen
April 1992—Evanston, Illinois

Peter, thirteen years old, is a good student but a reluctant reader who reads more for his mother's sake than for his own interest. Fantasy literature and comic books are his favorites. Unfortunately, at the public library there is only one book on the history of comics, which is often out. This has discouraged Peter from using the library to explore other materials and open up new areas of interest. He tells his mother there is more to read at the comic book store than at the library.

At school Peter was assigned a book report and asked to read a book of historical fiction. He went to the library and asked the librarian for help in choosing a book, telling her he liked knights, war, fighting, and adventure. She steered him in the direction of the fiction collection and offered three different books on civil war history. He tried to explain that he wanted something about knights, but she said this was all the library had.

After leaving the library Peter went to the comic book store and bought a book from the Dragon Lance series, which the teacher approved.

Have libraries changed in their service to youth in the last fifty-five years? Fortunately, they have. African-American youth have access to their local public library and can find help with their school work. Homework centers offer a welcoming environment to encourage teens to engage themselves in their school work.

Youths in some middle schools have the opportunity to help choose books for the collection. Others have talked with their favorite authors or published their own stories and poems. Affirmation and encouragement strengthen young people's interest in school, learning, and reading.

Employing students in both paying and non-paying positions in libraries not only helps young people develop good work habits and self-esteem, it also sends the message that the library is an important agency in the community that cares about the future of the next generation of readers and users.

The fact that the Margaret Alexander Edwards Recognition Awards for Exemplary Service to Youth exist indicates that youth services are alive and well. Mary K. Chelton, who edited this publication, says her faith in young adult services has been renewed after learning about the wonderful programs described here. It is our hope that library directors, librarians, and youth library "customers" use the descriptions of these exemplary programs as ideas for starting programs in their own communities.

CAROL S. NIELSEN

Acknowledgments

The ALA presidency has offered me a once-in-a-lifetime opportunity to focus on the issues in which I have always been professionally interested and involved: youth services, library services to young people at-risk, and outreach services. The generous grant of the Margaret Alexander Edwards Trust, culminating in this publication, has enabled me to fulfill one of my professional dreams: to focus the library's attention on the need to provide quality library service to youth. Customer service is the heart of the library and our youth are the heart of America. The top fifty programs included in this publication are recognized for the impact that they have had on the lives of young people.

I would like to thank all the librarians who submitted their programs for consideration by the President's Committee on Customer Service to Youth. Even those who did not win official recognition demonstrate that there is an active and vital interest in providing library services to youth.

The President's Committee on Customer Service to Youth, including Connie Champlin, Ray Fry, Sue Galloway, Sylvia Mavrogenes, and Sandra Payne, provided a terrific experience in working with professionals who are dedicated to spreading the news on quality library services for youth. In particular I would like to thank Ray Fry for encouraging me to undertake this project and steering me to the Margaret Alexander Edwards Trust for funding; Mary K. Chelton for her expertise as an editor, thinker, and young adult services advocate; Ann Kepler, whose help in editing and rewriting has made this publication more readable; and the ALA staff, including Peggy Sullivan, Linda Waddle, Bonnie Smothers, Mary Huchting, Dianne M. Rooney, Donavan Vicha, Harriet Banner, David Epstein, and Art Plotnik, all of whom contributed to the success of this project.

Finally, I thank Carol Nielsen for guiding this project from start to finish. She has offered me invaluable and solid support in the past two years.

My gratitude and thanks to all who have made this a successful, rewarding, and exciting project.

HARDY R. FRANKLIN
President
American Library Association

Introduction

The Contemporary Young Adult Library Customer

It is common knowledge that in the last twenty years the population of the American city has changed. In the past the public library catered to the well-heeled middle class to which most of us belonged. Today most of these people have fled the city, leaving behind the poor, the disadvantaged, the culturally deprived. Instead of college-bound, well-fed, well-mannered young people, we have thousands of adolescents who live in ghettos on relief, without a father and with a mother who never finished third grade. In their homes these people are unlikely to hear what we think of as interesting conversation. There is little mention of good taste, little talk of ethical standards. Too many of them drop out of school, commit crimes, take dope, join mobs, and hate all authority and established institutions. These conditions have made little difference in the public library's mode of procedure. The books are still on the shelves for those who wish to borrow them. This method, which never was too successful with the middle classes, is doomed to failure with the masses. Our new social crisis calls for new solutions.—*Margaret Alexander Edwards*[1]

Young adults of the last decade of the twentieth century are part of the thirteenth generation of Americans. They are the most diverse generation ever to come of age here—ethnically, culturally, and economically—but also the first in a century who are unlikely to surpass their parents' standard of living. There are relatively fewer of them than of the age cohorts who came before them, because Americans are now living longer and having fewer children. They are often characterized by others variously as cynical, apathetic, uninformed, undereducated, unhealthy, lazy, amoral, avaricious, sexist, racist, or violent. When adults are asked during youth-work training sessions, after being "helped" to remember their own adolescence through memory exercises, whether they would like to be an adolescent today instead of then, the answer is invariably a resounding *No!* Everyone seems to recognize that it is much more difficult to grow up today than it was for previous generations. That change is well characterized in a recent cartoon entitled *High School Sweethearts,* showing three YA couples, one each from 1950, 1970, and 1990. The captions read, "Let's get married first" (1950), "Let's get stoned first" (1970), and "Let's get tested first" (1990). Some go so far as to label today's young adults an entire generation at risk, and others write some of them off entirely.[2]

While cataclysmic assumptions of doom for the young have been around since Aristotle's time, it is fair to say that today's young adults are truly needier than those of earlier generations, in large part because of the demographic and economic changes that these "13ers" have inherited. The most profound of these changes have taken place within the family itself, namely, the increased labor-force participation of mothers, the rise in single-parent families because of divorce or births to never-married women, and the decline in real wages for men because of lost manufacturing jobs. The impact of these changes is increased for youth because they are more likely to live in poverty in households headed by women. Their access to adults, especially to successful male role models, has been greatly decreased by the absence of fathers and by the competing time-related stresses of parental lives. Both of these factors have given this generation more unsupervised time than previous generations had. Another result of family change is a lingering lack of faith in lasting relationships among the adolescent children of divorced parents. Some of the impoverished single-parent households are headed by young-adult females themselves. With many YAs literally raising themselves these days, the rise in gang activity universally reported is probably inevitable rather than remarkable.[3]

Although most of today's young adults have engaged in sexual activity long before graduating from high school, and many of them in urban areas have seen friends and family members murdered, there is persistent adult interest in protecting them from access to words, music, and images that various groups feel are bad for them or that they feel will induce adolescents to emulate the inappropriate behavior represented. Televised violence, the occult, alternative lifestyles, depictions of sexuality, and rap music continue to be of concern, regardless of whether overt censorship attempts take place or not.[4]

The fastest-growing group of this multicultural adolescent population is Hispanic. This group has, on the average, both the lowest levels of educational attainment and, at 35 percent, the highest number of school dropouts. But problems of educational attainment affect other youth as well. Despite some gains in reading scores for less-advantaged students and slightly improved mathematics proficiency, educational inequalities continue to exist. International comparisons lead many educators to doubt whether current academic achievement levels for any American students are high enough to ensure future American competitiveness.[5]

The leading causes of death among young adults are motor vehicle accidents, homicide and suicide. While many adolescent health problems can be attributed to lack of access to health care, many can also be attributed to a developmental propensity for risk-taking behavior, such as the use of drugs and the prevalence of guns. All health indicators are worse for those of lower socioeconomic status, who are disproportionately people of color because of racial and ethnic disparities in family income.[6]

Too many American schools are still preparing adolescents for a working world that is fast disappearing. Fields such as transportation, utilities, communications, government, and agriculture once offered steady employment to millions of young high school graduates. These jobs are disappearing, replaced by new jobs in the retail and service sectors at only half the wages. Those who graduate from high school but do not go on to college, sometimes called "the forgotten half," can rarely find a job that pays enough for them to leave their parents' home, let alone start their own families. The college bound may find their opportunities diminished as the downsizing of many American corporations and the loss of white-collar jobs send shock waves through the ranks of their parents.[7]

By 1989 only 40 percent of young adults in grades nine through twelve used computers in school, although teenage proficiency with computers is well reflected in the sales and popularity of video computer games. Young adults also participate in, and in some cases moderate, electronic bulletin boards on the Internet. Media images of teenage computer hackers, however, usually portray them as hacker outlaws, prompting a member of the Computer Professionals for Social Responsibility recently to suggest a national award for computer programmers under age eighteen in recognition of a valuable national intellectual resource. Automation and technology are ubiquitous in the everyday lives of adolescents, if only as part of their entertainment instead of their education.[8]

Despite all these changes, young adults still have a core group of developmental needs that must be addressed if they are to grow up to be functioning adults. These were outlined by Gisela Konopka at the University of Minnesota over twenty years ago, and they are as true for "13ers" as for their predecessors. She said that

> conditions for healthy development should provide young people with opportunities to participate as citizens, as members of a household, as workers, as responsible members of society;
>
> to gain experience in decision making;
>
> to interact with peers and acquire a sense of belonging;
>
> to reflect on self in relation to others and to discover self by looking outward as well as inward;
>
> to discuss conflicting values and formulate their own value system;
>
> to experiment with their own identity, with relationships to other people, with ideas; to try out various roles without having to commit themselves irrevocably;
>
> to develop a feeling of accountability in the context of a relationship among equals;
>
> to cultivate a capacity to enjoy life.

Given these conditions, adolescents will be enabled to gain experience in forming relationships and making meaningful commitments. They are not expected by the adult world to make final lifelong commitments; the expectation is related to their own need for interdependence and humanity's need for their commitment to others without losing themselves.[9]

Because of the developmental, informational, and social needs of today's young adults, it is important for the library community to

---

And those of us who are privileged to work with the formative period of adolescence have magnificent opportunities. Sometimes we are too close to the work to believe this . . . our work has to be done on faith and the unseen results confidently believed in. Youth's period of impressionability may be as brief as a New York spring . . . , but let us go on believing it is there and see to it that the marks we put upon it shall be the kind we are glad to recognize as our own in later years.

Amelia Munson[10]

---

realize how valuable a contribution libraries can make to the healthy development of young adults. While answering reference questions and circulating books for schoolwork and personal pleasure are worthy activities, they fall far short, not only of what is needed by adolescents, but also of what is possible. It has been a pleasure editing the descriptions of programs of librarians across the country who understand what is needed and how to do it. As the great science fiction writer Orson Scott Card said in Atlanta, "Young people know what they are hungry for. The librarian's job is to prepare the feast and set the banquet table." In that regard, this collection of programs represents a gourmet cookbook of library ideas for serving the contemporary young adult customer.

Young Adult Services

Young adults make up 25 percent of public library users and 99.9 percent of the users of secondary school libraries (which do serve a few teachers and staff). They also account for an unknown percentage of prison and institutional library users. Whether or not a library purports to have young adult services—an unfortunate term that is often understood only as a formal public library organizational response to their presence—adolescents are already in libraries in droves, with many more on the edges who could benefit from good library service. On the basis of the collection of top programs included in this publication, it may be helpful to discuss what contemporary service to young adults now includes, as well as what still needs to be included.[11]

When Anne Carroll Moore became concerned in the early part of the twentieth century about what happened to her adolescent users of the children's room when they were ready for the adult sections of the New York Public Library, she hired Mabel Williams to start what is now New York Public Library's Office of Work with Young Adults. Margaret Edwards visited Williams to get ideas for replicating the service at the Enoch Pratt Free Library in Baltimore. The idea of offering a transition entry and buffer into adult reading and collections is a strong core component of this service still. Indianapolis–Marion County uses this rationale for the video book commercials made by young teenagers as part of their summer reading club activities. Tucson-Pima extends this idea with a program that prepares older elementary school children for their passage into junior high school, an institution that did not exist in Moore's day but can often be just as unnerving for today's kids as the adult department of New York Public was for hers.[12]

Another reason Moore started a separate service for the young-adult age group was the anticipation of their school-related demands as high schools became established and affordable to ordinary young people. Public libraries are still responding to school-related needs in the San Diego (Calif.), Austin (Tex.), and Lincoln City (Nebr.) libraries' homework centers; the Monroe County (Ind.) Public Library's drop-in math tutoring program; and in Riverside City and County (Calif.) Library's outreach program in two middle schools. Cooperation between schools and public libraries has reached new levels, however, thanks to current computer and telecommunications technology. This sophisticated interagency networking on behalf of young adult users is exemplified by Capital City

Libraries (Alaska) and the Edmond (Okla.) Memorial High School Library Media Center.

A universal aspect of young-adult services has always been guidance to improve reading for personal enrichment and independent learning. Booktalks have always been used as one of the premiere means of telling kids about books and getting them excited about reading. The Miami-Dade (Fla.) Public Library System's outreach program to ninth graders, which includes booktalks, is as much a direct descendant of the early YA pioneers as are the booktalks of the West Baton Rouge (La.) Parish Library, the videotaped booktalk minidramas by the LAB group in Broward County (Fla.), and the peer booktalks of the District of Columbia Public Library's Youth Exchange program. Young-adult librarians, however, have always been very inventive about reading promotion, whether exemplified by the Lifelong Reader program in Greenville (S.C.) Middle School; the year-long, schoolwide River Valley (Ind.) Middle School Media Center program; the Brown County (Wis.) Public Library's YA summer reading club; the Oliver B. Wolcott (Conn.) Library's Civil War series; the meet-the-author programs of the Richmond (Va.) and Wichita (Kans.) school systems; or those of the Detroit Public Library and Langston Hughes Middle School of Fairfax County, Va.[13]

The training and level of staff delivering service to young adults have always been pivotal to serving adolescents successfully. Many of the contact people in these projects are role models for the kind of staff one searches for. In fact, when reading about the comprehensive programs in Mesa (Ariz.) Public Library and Fort Bend (Tex.) County Libraries, one wonders when these people sleep, but as the Berkeley (Calif.) Public Library's Staff Day program and the Washington State Young Adult Review Group demonstrate, that kind of staff can also be created with ingenuity, persistence, and the help of the young adults themselves.[14]

It has always been part of the young adult services concept (as well as the view of the larger youth-work community of which YA services are a part) that the young adults themselves must participate in the conceptualization and service-delivery process if the service is going to work. In recent years, librarians serving young adults have come to realize that this participation by youth is an experiential learning service in and of itself, regardless of the use of library materials. Youth participation gives young adults role rehearsal experiences, uses their intense developmental need for social experiences with peers, offers opportunities to employ their fledgling hypothetical thinking abilities, and channels their enormous emotional and physical energies into helping other people through helping the library. Whether it is the Salado (Tex.) Middle School Library's STARS, the B.B. Comer Library (Ala.) Teen Advisory Council, the Broward County (Fla.) Public Library's LAB, the New York Public Library's mural painters, the Mesa (Ariz.) Public Library's YAAC, the River Valley (Ind.) Middle School's Book Buddies, the middle school billboard artists in the Boston (Mass.) Public Library's promotional program, the twenty-five-member youth advisory board in West Baton Rouge (La.) Parish Library, or the young adolescent video producers in Indianapolis-Marion County (IN) Public Library, youth participation is still an intrinsic but also an expanding part of exemplary YA services programs.[15]

As Miriam Braverman points out in *Youth, Society and the Public Library,* "the pioneers in young adult services were champions of youth. They appreciated the anomalous position of young adults in society." She also documents two specific trends within the development of the service concept—the cultural and the social. The cultural trend included the reading-promotion and school-needs activities mentioned above. The social trend, on the other hand, aimed to "help young people understand and cope with conditions of life." She felt that the social trend was abandoned in the 1950s in favor of school visits and booktalking, but the programs recorded here make it clear that she was wrong. There is a constant strand of programs designed for young adults at risk, whether they are the three Blue Skies for Library Kids projects in the Chicago Public Library, the Alameda County (Calif.) Public Library System's Youth-at Risk project in its San Lorenzo Branch, Emporia (Kans.) Public Library's African-American male discussion programs, the DeKalb County (Ga.) Public Library's literacy program for teenage mothers, or the Wymore (Fla.) Career Education Center's children's literature program. Even the Austin (Tex.) Public Library's tutoring programs and homework centers were begun in response to poor local educational indicators and failing schools.[16]

The social trend in YA services is also present in the Rowan (N.C.) Public Library's jobs workshop program, New Iberia Parish (La.) Library's summer workshops, the Monroe County (Ind.) Books and Snacks at-risk program, and in the Miami-Dade (Fla.) program on black leaders. Nor are institutionalized teenagers forgotten, as demonstrated by the King County (Wash.) Youth Services Center library and also by the Cuyahoga County (Ohio) Project Leap kits. The increasingly pressing need for young adults to be comfortable with technology is answered by projects like the Muscatine (Iowa) and Cedar Shoals (Ga.) High School Media Center information programs. The need for recognition and self-expression is met by the New York Public Library's Youth Board on Staten Island. If young adult services turned inward in the 1950s, they have definitely turned around since.

There are also some persistently troubling aspects of services to young adults present here as well. The audience for these services is not consistently defined across libraries. The adolescent audience for these programs ranges in age from ten to twenty-one. This wide range is explained partly by the differences between ongoing and single programs and partly by the organizational origin of the program, but the disparities do make defining the services overall more difficult. It is obvious, though, that the entire age range of adolescence is covered by these self-nominated YA programs, so that even if a particular library narrows its definition of *young adult* for specific institutional reasons, such a narrow definition need not be generalized.

Young-adult service providers have always preferred action to writing reports, and the evaluation component of many of these programs is weaker than it should be. In some cases where numerical measures are used, their relationship to the program's objectives is unclear. While this vagueness is obviously part of a deadline-driven application process, the use of the word *approximately* should be struck from library reports forever. Luckily, two manuals to help librarians understand, use, and report evaluation measures are now available from the University of Wisconsin's Evaluating Library Programs and Services Project. They are *Evaluating Library Programs & Services: TELL IT!* and the *Evaluating Library Programs and Services: TELL IT! Training Manual* drawn from the insights of the two hundred librarians who attended the university's 1993 evaluation institutes. These two new manuals are in addition to

those on output measures published by the ALA.

It is obvious that good ideas for serving this age group are limited neither to a type of library nor to a particular part of the library organization. The staffing patterns are as varied as the YA age definitions. In fact, several programs demand the energies of multiple types of staff because the programs cross conventional age, grade level, or functional staffing lines. While this ad hoc staffing may make many wonder how ongoing services can be maintained under such an arrangement, the obvious commitment of resources and the response of the YA audience to many of these programs are very hopeful signs.

It has been a pleasure to meet these librarians through the editing of their program applications and to know that young adults are greatly cared for in many places around the country. If these programs inspire replication elsewhere, recognizing them here will have been more than worth it.

MARY K. CHELTON
Associate Editor
Voice of Youth Advocates

Sources

1. Margaret Alexander Edwards, *The Fair Garden and the Swarm of Beasts: The Library and the Young Adult* (New York: Hawthorn, 1969; reprint, Chicago: ALA, 1994).

2. Neil Howe and Bill Strauss, *13th Gen: Abort, Retry, Ignore, Fail?* (New York: Vintage, 1993); William Raspberry, "The Irredeemable," *Liberal Opinion* 5 (January 17, 1994): 5.

3. Joan S. Lipsitz, *After School: Young Adolescents on Their Own* (Carrboro, N.C.: Center for Early Adolescence, 1986); Task Force on Youth Development and Community Programs, *A Matter of Time: Risk and Opportunity in the Nonschool Hours* (New York: Carnegie Corporation of New York, 1992); Arland Thornton and Deborah Freedman, "The Changing American Family," *Population Bulletin* 38 (October, 1983); Barbara Dafoe Whitehead, "Dan Quayle Was Right," *Atlantic Monthly* 271 (April, 1993): 47.

4. U.S. Congress, Office of Technology Assessment, *Adolescent Health,* vol. 1, *Summary*

and Policy Options, OTA-H-468 (Washington, D.C.: U.S. Government Printing Office, 1991); Children's Express, *Voices from the Future: Our Children Tell Us about Violence in America,* edited by Susan Goodwillie (New York: Crown, 1993); *Newsletter on Intellectual Freedom* (Chicago: ALA, bimonthly).

5. William O'Hare, "How Children Are Changing," *American Demographics* 14 (February, 1992): 36-42; Jonathan Kozol, *Savage Inequalities* (New York: Crown, 1991); *Youth Indicators 1993: Trends in the Well-Being of American Youth,* Washington, D.C.: National Center for Education Statistics, 1993; U.S. Department of Education, *America 2000: An Education Strategy,* rev. ed. (Washington, D.C.: U.S. Government Printing Office, 1991).

6. *Adolescent Health,* vol. 1, *Summary and Policy Options.*

7. *Youth Indicators,* 1993; Commission on Work, Family and Citizenship, *The Forgotten Half: Non-College Youth in America* (Washington, D.C.: William T. Grant Foundation, 1988).

8. *CPSR Newsletter* (Winter, 1993), reprinted in *VOYA* 16 (August, 1993): 3.

9. "Requirements for the Healthy Development of Adolescent Youth," *Adolescence* 8 (Fall, 1973): 1–26.

10. Amelia Munson, *Books and Young People: An Ample Field* (Chicago: ALA, 1950).

11. *Services and Resources for Young Adults in Public Libraries* (Washington, D.C.: National Center for Education Statistics, 1988).

12. Mabel Williams, personal interview, 1979.

13. Sister Marie Inez Johnson, "The Development of Separate Service for Young People in Public Libraries of the United States, and Its Implications for Library Schools," M.L.S. thesis, Columbia University, 1940.

14. Edwards, *Fair Garden.*

15. U.S. Department of Health, Education, and Welfare, National Commission on Resources for Youth, *An Introductory Manual on Youth Participation for Program Administrators,* DHEW Publication OHD/OYD/76-26045 (Washington, D.C.: U.S. Government Printing Office, n.d.); *Youth Participation in Libraries: A Training Manual* (Chicago: Young Adult Library Services Association (formerly YASD)/ALA, 1989).

16. Miriam Braverman, *Youth, Society, and the Public Library* (Chicago: ALA, 1979).

President's Committee for Customer Service to Youth

The following persons comprise the committee involved in the planning and execution of this book:

Constance Champlin, MSD Washington Township School District, 3801 East 79th Street, Indianapolis, IN 46240-3407

Mary K. Chelton, Associate Editor (ex officio), *Voice of Youth Advocates,* Scarecrow Press, 52 Liberty Street, Metuchen, NJ 08840

Hardy R. Franklin, Director, District of Columbia Public Library, 901 G. Street, NW, Washington, DC 20021

Ray M. Fry, Director, Library Programs, U.S. Department of Education, Office of Educational Research and Improvement, 555 New Jersey Avenue, NW, Washington, DC 20208-5571

Sue Galloway, Librarian, Oklahoma School for the Deaf, E. 10th and Tahlequah, Sulphur, OK 73086-3045

Sylvia Mavrogenes, Youth Services Administrator, Miami-Dade Public Library System, 101 West Flagler Street, Miami, FL 33130-1523

Sandra Payne, Young Adult Librarian, New York Public Library Branches, Staten Island Borough Office, 5 Central Avenue, Staten Island, NY 10301-2501

ALA Staff Liaisons

Carol Nielsen, Office of the President

Linda Waddle, Young Adult Library Services Association

Bonnie Smothers, Acquisitions Editor

American Library Association
50 East Huron Street
Chicago, IL 60611

The Top Ten

1.
Alameda County Public Library

Fremont, California

Idea

Multifaceted Youth-at-Risk Outreach Project

Customers

Young adults, ages thirteen through nineteen

Setting

The San Lorenzo Branch of the Alameda County Library serves a population of 47,665 in the unincorporated communities of San Lorenzo, Ashland, and Cherryland, California. There are 2,962 youth in grades eight through twelve in the San Lorenzo Unified School District. Fifty percent of these youth are of multicultural heritage including 23 percent Hispanic-American, 17 percent Asian-American, 8 percent African-American, and 2 percent Native American. Between 1980 and 1989 there was a 22 percent increase in the number of children living in Alameda County in extreme poverty, and a 64 percent increase in school-age children whose families received Aid for Families with Dependent Children (AFDC). The school dropout rate was 11.7 percent, and births to teenage mothers increased by 35.5 percent between 1985 and 1988. In 1990 30 percent of all gonorrhea cases and 8.6 percent of all syphilis cases reported were youth between fifteen and nineteen.

Program Description

A Youth-at-Risk Outreach Project was designed from a survey of youth and youth-service providers in the San Lorenzo service area during the summer of 1991. The needs assessment survey was accomplished through twelve teen focus groups, eleven key informant interviews, and questionnaires. Through this process, the library found that the greatest needs of youth were those directly related to jobs and job skills, multicultural relations, health and sexuality, and awareness of community and library resources available to youth. In addition, every focus group and one-third of the informants expressed a need for community recreation programs and facilities for teenagers. Service providers were also concerned about the lack of family stability.

In response to the survey, a Youth-At-Risk Steering Committee was formed, which included teenagers and staff from education and social service agencies. Its task was to determine how the library could effectively meet youth needs in an ongoing way. Four goals were chosen:

1. To increase youth awareness of library resources
2. To provide interactive, informational forums for young adults that address key issues identified in the needs assessment
3. To increase understanding and communication between library staff and community young adults
4. To work cooperatively with community organizations and agencies to heighten awareness of youth-at-risk issues

The underlying goal of the entire program was to reach youth who did not typically view the library as a "cool" place to go, to help them realize the many ways in which the library could help them, and to eliminate the image of the library as a necessary evil mandated by school assignments.

Seven youth forums collaboratively planned by library staff, community members, and a YA consultant group were held. Topics ranged from job opportunities and interviewing skills, cultural sensitivity, and sexuality and relationships to a "rap against racism" program by local rappers. Two informational brochures, entitled "For Y.A.s Only!" and "Young Adult Resource Guide: San Lorenzo Area," were produced and distributed.

Funding

The program obtained an LSCA grant of $37,710, which included $975 for duplicating and printing, $1,500 for library materials, $3,500 for contract personnel, $400 for refreshments, and $1,500 for equipment. This was matched by an in-kind contribution of $29,835 by the library, which included $1,000 for duplicating and printing, $9,800 for library materials, and $19,035 for salaries.

Contact Persons

Gary Morrison or Caryn Sipos, Alameda County Library, 2450 Stevenson Boulevard, Fremont, CA 94538. (510) 745-1492 (Morrison); (510) 670-6282 (Sipos)

Pocket-size resource guide with relevant phone numbers.

Alameda County Library

Young Adult Resource Guide San Lorenzo Area

24 HOUR CRISIS LINES
AIDS Hotline..............................1-800-FOR-AIDS
Alameda County Child Protective Services 483-9300
Alameda County Health Care Services......................... 677-7800
Alameda County Psychiatric Emergency...................... 534-8055
Bay Area Women Against Rape 845-RAPE
California Youth Crisis Line.............................. 834-5200
Poison Control Center....................................476-6600
Suicide Prevention.......................................889-1333
ALCOHOL & DRUGS
Al-Anon/Alateen 276-2270
Alcoholics Anonymous.....................................886-2123
Narcotics Anonymous 843-3701
Second Chance...886-8696
Thunder Road 653-5040

CHILD CARE REFERRAL
4 C's 582-2189
Davis Street Center.....................................635-8500
COUNSELING
Birthright ("Pro-Life")................................. 839-9203
Birthways...464-3095
Crisis Pregnancy Center ("Pro-Life").....................487-4357
Eden Children's Center 667-7540
Family Service of the East Bay.......................... 887-1843
Girl's Inc., Hayward.................................... 887-0113
Girl's Inc., San Leandro................................ 357-5515
Hayward Youth & Family Service 784-7048
La Familia Counseling Service............................881-5921
Pathways Counseling Center..............................357-5515
Project Eden..887-0566
San Leandro Community Counseling.........................638-6603
Southern Alameda County YWCA............................785-2736

GAY & LESBIAN YOUTH
Pacific Center for Human Growth......................... 841-6224
HEALTH
AIDS Project of the East Bay............................834-8181
Clinic for Adults and Children.........................483-4550
Hayward Community Health Center 667-5300
Miranda Clinic 786-6517
Native American Clinic 261-8943
Planned Parenthood......................................733-1814
Tiburcio Vasquez Clinic 783-5360
Tri-City Clinic...797-1188

more on back . . .

2.
B. B. Comer Memorial Public Library

Sylacauga, Alabama

Idea

Teen Advisory Council

Customers

Young adults, ages twelve through eighteen

Setting

The B. B. Comer Memorial Library is a municipal library serving the 12,500 residents of the town of Sylacauga, as well as those within a thirty-mile radius from Talladega, Clay, Coosa, Shelby, and Tallapoosa Counties in rural northeastern Alabama. The population of this section of the state is about 27 percent African-American, with an average per capita income of $24,280, which is lower than the state average. Approximately six thousand young adults live in the service areas. The 21,000-square-foot building is open seven days a week, 350 days a year, and houses over seventy thousand books, 175 periodicals, and an array of other materials. Since the inception of the Teen Advisory Council (TAC), the library has a designated young-adult area of approximately three thousand square feet with materials, tables, and carrels.

Program Description

The Teen Advisory Council (TAC), started in 1989 with the encouragement of Christy Tyson, then at the Alabama State Library, consists of twelve to fifteen young adults from city and county schools who help to plan and promote programs for their age group,

publicize the library, share their talents with younger children through booktalking, keep a readers' advisory notebook in the YA Department for their peers, and contribute to a newsletter and book lists. The TAC meets once a month—more often when necessary. The group fosters friendship among teens from different schools, races, and socioeconomic groups, as well as benefiting their peers who live in the service area. Current objectives include reading and studying the following:

1. Censored books and authors
2. The environment, with related clean-up projects such as cleaning a block every month
3. The problems of aging, with a connected project of visiting nursing homes during the holidays
4. The problems of the poor and homeless, with an adopt-a-family project
5. Booktalking at each TAC meeting to keep the readers' advisory notebook current

Funding

Started with two LSCA grants of $8,159 (1989) and $6,850 (1990), the council is now supported by the regular library budget.

Contact Person

Tracey Crumpton, Youth Services Director, B. B. Comer Memorial Library, 314 North Broadway Avenue, Sylacauga, AL 35150. (205) 249-0961

Christy Tyson with the first TAC group.

3.
Berkeley Public Library

Berkeley, California

Idea

In-service staff training day about young adult customers

Customers

Public library system staff of 124

Setting

The Berkeley Public Library serves the city of Berkeley with a Central Library, four neighborhood branch libraries, and a Tool Lending Library. Its 210 employees fill 120.13 full-time equivalent positions to serve ninety-two thousand registered borrowers. The library is open sixty-four hours a week and experiences more than 1.4 million visits annually. The library serves a population of 104,200 (60 percent Caucasian-American, including a large foreign community, 20 percent African-American, 14 percent Asian-American, 9 percent Hispanic-American). Just under 10 percent of the population is of school age (five to seventeen years old). There is a wide range of income levels in this university community, and about 16 percent of the community lives below the poverty line. In 1989 the library institutionalized young adult services with the hiring of five young-adult librarians, one for each branch and one for Central. YA services include special collections, system-wide programming and site-specific projects. The annual materials budget for young adult books and music is $14,000. Programs are funded by gift money from the Friends of the Library.

Program Description

In 1992 the YA librarians suggested an in-service staff day about teenagers so that staff could become better informed about behavioral issues and the role of the library in teens' lives. The director received board permission to close all facilities one Friday morning so that all staff could attend. The four hours of training, planned by the senior librarian for young adult services, one branch YA librarian, and the library's special services coordinator, were intended to offer all staff some "insight on teenagers' lives so that we can serve them better . . . at the library and . . . feel more comfortable at home, on our streets, and in all the other places we . . . share with them." Planning focused on three substantive issues: the physical ramifications of adolescence, the social world of youth, and the political tensions between the institutional library and teens.

Invited to address the issues were two adult experts—a nurse practitioner in adolescent medicine and the city high school's curriculum developer and lead teacher of the required multicultural studies course. Speakers also included a panel of eighteen teenagers representing all strata of the teen public. Each teenage panelist was invited to bring along a friend as an adjunct panelist or for moral support. Both adults and teenagers were paid an honorarium and completed the library's standard volunteer form. A student worker prepared a personalized packet for each presenter, who also received a T-shirt, designed by a young artist and library patron, to commemorate the day.

The 124 registered staff were then divided into discussion groups so that no one would be with his or her immediate supervisor and so that each group evenly represented staff titles, gender, ethnicity, and likelihood of energetic participation. Three teen panelists were placed with each small group. Each of the YA librarians, along with the high school teacher, served as a facilitator during the small-group discussions with teen panel members.

Before staff day the panelists met to acquaint themselves with each other and the YA librarians and to review everyone's expectations. The facilitators were reminded to protect the teen panelists from any harassing or embarrassing questions. It was emphasized with both panel and staff that panelists must be treated with respect and courtesy.

On staff day the adults gave their presentations before the mid-morning break. The panelists arrived during the break and were offered refreshments before going onstage. During the panel's first half hour, the teens introduced themselves, and many offered views of the library (both wildly positive and politely negative). Some willingly fielded staff questions, and the discussions continued for forty-five minutes in the small groups, where both teens and staff offered many suggestions for new or refurbished services. Ninety-three completed evaluations showed that the teens were the most popular part of the day. The nurse was more popular than the teacher, but only five staff members wanted information they had not perceived as available during the training.

In the weeks and months after the training, staff have continued to discuss staff day; they have often asked YA staff to address some issues, like particular program ideas, immediately. Public-service staff now recognize certain teen behaviors (for example, clumsiness and eating) as part of the physical adolescent growth process rather than an outbreak of delinquency. Technical-services staff act on their renewed understanding that materials requested by teens are no less valuable to their users despite teenage tastes. All staff seem eager to discuss perceived teen needs and problems with the YA staff, whose jobs they now better understand. Word that teens had been invited to speak to the staff got around town and renewed credibility for the library in teenagers' eyes.

Funding

Support comprised $2,595 from the library director's discretionary fund ($925 for speakers, $1,400 for T-shirts, $160 for refreshments, $30 for paper goods, and $80 for staff equipment setup).

Each staff member who attended the training received a T-shirt.

Contact Person

Francisca Goldsmith, Senior Librarian, Berkeley Public Library, 2090 Kittredge Street, Berkeley, CA 94704. (510) 649-3926

4.
Cedar Shoals High School Learning Resources Center

Athens, Georgia

Idea

Information services to help students become lifelong learners who are information literate; School Library Media Center Advisory Committee of teachers, students, and parents

Customers

High school students, grades nine through twelve

Setting

Cedar Shoals, a grade-nine-to-twelve comprehensive high school, was opened in 1972 in the eastern sector of Clarke County. The school population of approximately fifteen hundred students is drawn largely from Athens and the surrounding area as well as the community of Winterville, located about seven miles from the University of Georgia campus. Students are bused in from the northeastern area of the county as well. The student population is approximately 48 percent Caucasian-American, 48 percent African-American, and 4 percent a combination of Hispanic-American, Asian-American, and Native American. A large percentage of the students is upper middle class, with parents employed by the university; however, another large percentage of the student population lives at or below the poverty level, as evidenced by the 32 percent who qualify for free or reduced-cost lunches.

Program Description

The Learning Resources Center (LRC), with two media specialists and one half-time aide, assists fifteen hundred students and an instructional staff of one hundred in using information in print, audiovisual, and electronic media. Students can use an electronic catalog to retrieve information from a collection encompassing print materials, filmstrips, art slides, videos, computer programs, and transparencies. The computerized network provides access from classrooms to the media center catalog as well as online access to the University of Georgia Libraries and Athens Regional Library. Networked and stand-alone CD-ROM stations provide a variety of information access, including *WilsonDisc, Grolier's Multimedia Encyclopedia, Granger's Index to Poetry, Discovering Authors,* and *Microsoft Bookshelf Reference Library for Windows.* A School Library Media Center Advisory Committee of teachers, media specialists, administrators, students, and parents meets monthly to plan and coordinate the media program. Extended hours allow students additional time to use the center's resources.

Cooperative planning among teachers and media specialists is the core of the program to teach students to use library resources for information retrieval and independent research. Freshmen receive an orientation to the LRC at the beginning of the school year. Information-access skills are emphasized throughout the instructional program rather than being taught in isolation. Flexible scheduling allows for simultaneous use of the center as well as an open-access computer lab by an entire class, small groups, and individual students. Both Apple II and Macintosh computers are available in the lab. In addition to the MECC software collection, the LRC has teacher-selected CAI software and utility programs for word processing and desktop publishing.

Student and faculty input regarding purchases for the LRC is sought in a variety of ways, including approval of a budget by the Media Advisory Committee, a suggestion box in the center for students' book requests, and a "roundtable" materials selection held with each instructional department.

The Georgia Media Specialist Evaluation Program is the formal procedure for evaluating all media specialists and programs in Georgia. An administrator is involved in the formal process that includes observations and documentation checks as well as surveys of students and faculty. Results of last year's survey led to the purchase of another CD-ROM work station and eight new computers for the computer lab.

Funding

The center is supported primarily by state funds allotted each year ($19,000 in 1992–93), with at least one book fair each year to raise money (approximately $1,000) for extras. Five regular volunteers each help at least two hours a week, and other parent and student volunteers serve throughout the year for special projects such as the book fair. Parents and students also serve on the Media Advisory/Technology Committee.

Contact Persons

Dana McDougald and Sydney Lowry, Learning Resources Center, Cedar Shoals High School, 1300 Cedar Shoals Drive, Athens, GA 30610. (706) 546-5375

Some students using CD-ROMs. The nearest computer has *WilsonDisc* in it and the other has *Grolier's Encyclopedia*. Other available programs include *Bookshelf, Granger's Index to Poetry,* and *Discovering Authors.*

5.
Chicago Public Library

Chicago, Illinois

Idea

Male high school students serve as read-aloud partners for elementary school boys

Customers

Fifteen male high school students

Setting

The program is offered at the Hall and Robert Taylor Homes branches of the Chicago Public Library, located in the Grand Boulevard area of Chicago, the second poorest congressional district in the United States. This is an African-American community in which income is low, unemployment is high, crime is excessive, and housing is inadequate.

Program Description

The Male Mentoring/Read Aloud Program (RAP), part of CPL's Blue Skies for Library Kids Project, is a response to the community's expressed need for young males to have positive role models to help raise self-esteem as well as to the library's need to appeal to boys and find a means of creating programs collaboratively with community organizations and institutions.

Begun in the spring of 1993 in partnership with DuSable High School and the Chicago Children's Museum, RAP features fifteen high school students who spend two afternoons a week working one-on-one with young boys in the library. The boys take turns reading aloud to each other; the older boys help with homework, and they are launching a library chess club.

Read-aloud mentors were selected by a high school teacher-counselor. Younger children were recruited by the library staff. YA mentors were instructed by library staff on choosing appropriate materials. They were trained in storytelling and hands-on activities for children by the staff of the Chicago Children's Museum. Participants were invited to spend a special overnight at the museum as a reward for their hard work—the first time several of them had ever spent a night away from home.

Parents have expressed support for the program's success in keeping younger boys out of trouble and for improving study skills among the children and the young adults.

Funding

The Blue Skies for Library Kids Project is funded by a $1 million grant from the Chicago Community Trust through the Chicago Public Library Foundation. The grant supports projects in eighteen branches, of which this is one.

Contact Person

Regina Johnson, Hall Branch Library, 4801 South Michigan Avenue, Chicago, IL 60615. (312) 747-2541

6.
DeKalb County Public Library

Decatur, Georgia

Idea

An intergenerational literacy program for teen parents and their babies

Customers

Low-literate, at-risk young adults, fifteen through eighteen years old, who are parents of children ages birth through thirty-six months

Setting

DeKalb County, the second largest county in Georgia, encompasses a diverse urban population of close to six hundred thousand residents. The project was conducted at the Scottdale Child Development Center and the Crim High School Family Ties Child Development and Daycare Center.

Program Description

Building Blocks to Literacy was designed to reach teenage parents, ages fifteen through eighteen, to help them become their child's first teacher. Program objectives were:

1. To enroll twenty-four families
2. To provide four six-week sessions of programming within a year
3. To motivate 92 percent of the participants to involve their children independently in activities that lead to the development of language skills

During 1992–93, fifty-eight very young children were introduced to early literacy skills while librarians modeled methods of developing language and cognitive skills through play for forty-six parents. One hundred percent of the participating families reported reading, singing, and actively playing with their children on a regular basis as a result of the program, a 96 percent increase over preprogram levels.

Families attended a minimum of six weekly sessions, each of which was divided into forty-

Mothers—most of them teenagers— sat with infants thrown over their shoulders, toddlers sitting on the floor at their feet, preschoolers screaming distractedly and running in circles . . . the only words the mothers uttered were, "No! Don't! Stop that!" There was no one reading a book to a child; no conversation; no singing of lullabies to fretful infants.

I went away with the strong conviction that the library had to find a way to help these young moms learn the value of communication—the value of talking with their children.

*from a presentation
by Sherry Des Enfants
at the 1993 ALA Annual Conference*

five minutes of playtime while the librarian modeled how to talk to children; fifteen minutes of "circle time," during which the librarian led families in rhymes, songs, stories, and chants. Afterwards, the librarians supervised the children while the parents were tutored in ways to share books, rhymes, puppets, and stories.

Funding

A grant of $14,709 from the Barbara Bush Foundation for Family Literacy provided a half-time senior library assistant to conduct playtime and circle-time sessions, plus all toys, board books, and parenting materials used. Tutoring sessions were conducted by Literacy Volunteers of America. Meals were provided by a grant from the Decatur Chapter of the National Coalition of 100 Black Women.

Contact Person

Sherry Des Enfants, DeKalb County Public Library, 215 Sycamore Street, Decatur, GA 30030. (404) 370-8458

7.
Detroit Public Library

Detroit, Michigan

Idea

Special day to meet an author who has been selected and read in advance by young adults

Customers

Younger young adults, grades seven through nine

Setting

This program is available at eight branches and the Main Library of the Detroit Public Library System. The library has been in existence for nearly 130 years. Its Main Library, with 1.6 million books, is also a State Resource Library. There are twenty-five neighborhood branches, a Municipal Reference Library, and an SIR (Service to Shut-Ins and Retirees) program, as well as a variety of special services and collections. The program was initiated in 1987 at the Monteith Branch, located in one of the most socially, economically, and educationally depressed areas of Detroit. Participating students now represent the spectrum of socioeconomic backgrounds.

Program Description

Author Day is an annual, ongoing reading-incentive program to encourage recreational reading among young adults in grades seven through nine. It encompasses eight branches within the Detroit Public Library system and eighteen public and private schools. Organized by eight librarians from the participating branches, with the cooperation of enthusiastic and committed local teachers, the program includes the following activities.

Each student is expected to read at least three books from a preselected list of six YA titles, chosen for literary merit and appeal to the target age group, and to participate in class discussion about the books and their authors. Each student then completes an Author Day book-report form and votes for his or her favorite author. The winning writer is then invited to speak at the Author Day Grand Finale held at the Detroit Main Library and several branches.

All finale programs include dialogue with the winning author and mingling of students from various Detroit schools. Selected students also attend a luncheon with the author, public and school librarians, and participating teachers. The young adults learn about additional titles by the author and are given the opportunity to purchase one or more autographed copies.

Program evaluation includes the gathering of statistics on the number of books read, the number of young adults enrolled in the program, and the number qualifying to vote for their favorite author and attend the program. In 1993 some 1,100 students read over 5,000 books and qualified to meet author Walter Dean Myers. Previous authors have included Richard Peck, Joyce Carol Thomas, Ron Koertge, Gloria Miklowitz, and Cynthia Grant.

Walter Dean Meyers at the author day grand finale.

Funding

The most recent event, which cost $2,818.50, was fully funded by the Friends of the Detroit Public Library. Funding varies from $3,000 to $4,000, depending on the author's fee. Friends' funding pays all author and luncheon expenses. The Detroit Public Library provides all books, promotional materials, and record keeping. DPL's youth librarians are responsible for staff management.

Contact Person

Joanne Johnson, Librarian First Assistant, Hubbard Branch Library, Detroit Public Library, 12929 West McNichols, Detroit, MI 48235. (313) 935-3434

8.
Greenville Middle School

Greenville, South Carolina

Idea

Three-part Lifelong Readers Program including author interviews by phone, parents' participation in their young teenagers' reading experiences, and a morning read-aloud program for students who arrive early

Customers

Middle school students, grades six through eight, and their parents

Setting

Greenville Middle School is one of fifteen middle schools in the Greenville County School District, serving 730 students from a very diverse population ranging from upper middle class to those from federally subsidized homes. Approximately 30 percent of the student body is minority. The library media center is physically and philosophically "the center of the school."

Program Description

The Lifelong Readers Program has two active components that have been in place for over twenty years.

Dial-an-Author allows students the opportunity to interview writers of young-adult books by telephone. The interviews take place after the students have engaged in an extensive study of the works of a particular writer. There are no restrictions to this program; all students are offered the opportunity to participate, and teachers look forward to making this a part of their curriculum plans. To date, students have conducted over five hundred interviews with approximately two hundred different writers. Students have labeled this program a success and continue to read books by favorite writers long after the interviews have ended.

Communicate through Literature is the second component, designed to encourage parents to participate in their young teenagers' reading experiences. Parents are invited to the school library media center once a month for an hour of book discussion. They read books recommended by their middle schoolers and come to the meetings prepared to discuss their child's reading experiences. Students are not present at the parent meetings. The idea is to ask parents to read and discuss books with their children at home. Parents are issued patron cards and are encouraged to use the school's library media center for their family reading needs. As a result of the program's success, many parents who have children in other schools have called to ask if they can participate in the meetings. Participating parents now realize that reading can remain an important part of their family life during the children's teenage years.

Start the Day with a Book was added in 1992. This is a morning read-aloud program for students who arrive at school early. Approximately thirty students gathered before school in 1992 to hear ten complete novels read. In 1993 more than seventy students signed up. The students have been divided into two groups, with a language arts teacher volunteering to read to one group while the library media specialist reads to the other. This is strictly a recreational reading program involving students from all grades and ability levels. Parents have told staff that their young adults have rearranged car pools in an effort to get to school in time for morning reading. The program is such a success that there is a waiting list for the novels being read, even by students who cannot come to school early. The principal supports the program by relieving the teacher of traditional before- and after-school duties.

The Lifelong Readers Program unites the efforts of parents, teachers, and the library staff in promoting reading.

Funding

The PTA pays for the long-distance phone calls to interview authors. No costs are involved in the other programs beyond a commitment of the library media specialist's time.

Contact Person

Pat Scales, Library Media Specialist, Greenville Middle School, 339 Lowndes Avenue, Greenville, SC 29607. (803) 241-3363

9.
Monroe County Public Library

Bloomington, Indiana

Idea

Reading motivation through asking young adult help with selection

Customers

At-risk young adults, ages thirteen through twenty

Setting

Monroe County Library is a medium-sized library serving a county population of 108,978 (94.4 percent Caucasian American), of whom 6,125 are teens enrolled in six public secondary schools in 1992. The area's economy is service-based and focused on Indiana University. There is no large city within fifty miles. A young-adult librarian, hired in 1989 to serve young adults ages thirteen through twenty, organized ninety-eight programs and made eighty classroom presentations in 1992 to a combined audience of 4,216 young adults. This program took place in the Bloomington Parks and Recreation Department's Westside Community Center.

Program Description

Books and Snacks was a collaborative effort to encourage at-risk youth to read as part of their leisure-time activities. School and social services agencies identified participants and then referred them to the Westside Center's Positive Leisure among Youth (PLAY) program. The Books and Snacks objectives were to

1. Create a current and popular paperback collection at the center
2. Expand reading time and interests by asking the young adults to select the books
3. Increase the young adults' familiarity with and use of the public library
4. Involve the teenagers in promoting and continuing the program the following year

The program was set up in two five-week sessions that also included group-building activities and snacks. The project provided transportation from participants' schools to the library, where the teens were given exclusive access to a collection of 100 new paperback books and asked to help select new books for the Westside Center's library. They could spend $750 and the public library would match their purchases by adding another copy to the library's YA collection. To make a recommendation, a student had to read the book or a review. The students also planned and promoted a video book review and community celebration.

For the most part, the young adults were not good students; some did not read school-related material, nor were they fast or proficient readers. However, they all considered themselves readers! As the program developed, it became obvious that they needed to touch and hold the books, so several meetings were held at two local bookstores, where they were allowed to discuss and vote in the store. Before shopping, they worked out a buying plan and criteria for selection. The group made excellent choices, selected a well-balanced collection, and engaged in discussions that touched on censorship, literary quality, and responsibility and sensitivity to the community for whom the books were being selected.

Twenty-six middle school and high school students participated. All increased their use of the public library. Only one student had an active library card at the beginning of the project; none of the others had either applied for or used a card for the last five years. By the last meeting, these students had borrowed 150 books. One young man picked up a William Sleator novel and proceeded to read as many of Sleator's books as he could find. He is now reading Orson Scott Card, whom he discovered as he reviewed books in a book-buying session. The program widened the students' knowledge of different fiction genres as well as helping them to discover nonfiction as viable leisure reading. Libraries and bookstores became comfortable, inviting, and interesting places to spend time. The unveiling of the new book collection drew a hundred community, government, family, and neighborhood members.

Evaluation included tracking each student's attendance and participation in discussions. Participants' library cards were coded to record the number of books borrowed throughout the project. Staff discussions provided informal evaluation.

Funding

A $750 Lilly Endowment grant to the Indiana Library Federation was used to purchase the Westside collection. Costs for activities were covered by existing agency budgets. The Bloomington Parks and Recreation Department has deposited $300 in the public library's gift account to fund next year's purchases.

Contact Person

Dana Burton, Youth Services Librarian, Monroe County Public Library, 303 East Kirkwood Avenue, Bloomington, IN 47408. (812) 339-2271

Zranda Boyd, left, and Shalonda Winston, right, look at the new books they helped select for the Westside Community Center while Clay Merrifield reads up on Michael Jordan.

(Reprinted with permission of the *Herald Times*, Bloomington, Indiana. Photo by Tom Weis.)

10.
San Diego Public Library

San Diego, California

Idea

Homework centers

Customers

At-risk youth

Setting

The program was offered at public library branches and at satellite sites in recreation centers, YMCAs, Girls and Boys Clubs, and housing complexes within the city of San Diego.

Program Description

An integral part of the city's Neighborhood Pride and Protection Program (NPP), the homework centers in thirty-three public library branches, the central library, and seven satellite sites include specialized juvenile reference collections to help youth complete school assignments. Special subject materials have been added to support and enhance the schools' curricula. Study carrels give students a place to study, and computer workstations have been loaded with software to assist users in building math, geography, science, reading, and SAT skills. The computers may also be used to complete school reports or personal resumes. In addition, the centers offer tutoring services, which are neighborhood-based and sponsored by local area agencies. At most sites two to three volunteers help students with homework and literacy skills.

Satellite homework centers were created in seven communities plagued with alcohol and substance abuse and gang and criminal activities to support the library's extension and community outreach services. These sites were selected based on accessibility, level of youth activity, safety and security, space, volunteer staffing, and commitment to the NPP program. Each satellite center provides a core collection of reference materials and a volunteer tutoring program. Periodic visits are made by librarians to ensure that the satellite centers are running smoothly and to determine needs.

Monthly, 250 to 300 youth in each library service area utilize one or more of the services offered in the centers. Success is measured by computer use, matches of tutors and students, the condition of the collections and equipment, youth circulation, and a door count. An output measures survey is planned.

Peer tutoring at Valencia Park.

Funding

The program is funded through the city of San Diego's General Fund budget.

Contact Person

Francisco Pinneli, San Diego Public Library, 820 E Street, San Diego, CA 92101-6778. (619) 236-5863

Collaborative Efforts

11.
Boston Public Library

Boston, Massachusetts

Idea

A billboard ad contest on the theme of the Boston Public Library, books, readers, or reading; and a writing competition for high school students in conjunction with a library card registration campaign

Customers

Boston public school students in grades six through twelve, with special focus on grades seven and ten. (Historically, there has been a decline in library use at these grades.)

Setting

The program is offered at the Central Library and twenty-five branches of the Boston Public Library and the nine middle schools and sixteen high schools of the Boston Public School System.

Program Description

The Library-School Partnership Program was undertaken during the 1992–93 school year to strengthen the working relationship between the Boston Public Library and the Boston Public Schools and to increase students' knowledge and use of the public library through increased library-card registration and through two specific, high-visibility projects—a billboard ad contest and a writing competition. A description of the library-card campaign and special projects was sent to all principals by the school superintendent. Library-card registration and the billboard ad competition were decentralized to the local branch staff, who worked with local schools to link registrations to class visits in either location. In the Central Library Young Adult Department, YA authors William Sleator, Nancy Garden, and Sook Nyul Choi served as judges for the high school writing competition. The writing competition was preceded by a creative writing seminar conducted by two editors and a panel of teen writers from *Merlyn's Pen: The National Magazine of Student Writing*, to further promote the competition that young adult librarians and high school teachers were encouraging in the classrooms.

Results were announced at an awards ceremony in May. There were 55 winners out of 107 entries in the high school contest, and 5 winners out of 154 middle school participants. In addition to the year-long middle school billboard displays, the library published the high school winners in *Discovery: Award-Winning Writers in a Boston High School Competition* in August and registered nearly twenty thousand new young customers—a 30 percent one-year increase.

Funding

The Boston Public Library Foundation recruited donations. Ackerly Communications provided the use of 200 outdoor billboards for a one-year period for winning designs. Binney and Smith, manufacturers of Crayola crayons, donated crayons to middle school competitors. The

Westin Hotel contributed the catered awards ceremony. Catherine Clancy of the Central Library's Young Adult Department recruited the services of the young adult authors and the editorial staff of *Merlyn's Pen*.

Contact Person

Catherine Clancy, Boston Public Library, Young Adult Department, Copley Square, Boston, MA 02116. (617) 536-5400, ext. 334

I Remember

I remember my childhood. Yesterday
   When I believed in wishing upon the stars
   Believing my dreams were never far.
But those days never did last.

I remember how days were just days,
   How the sun rose
   And how it would set to a close.
Those days went by too fast.

I remember the fairy tales told by my father
   When he lifted me up on his lap and
   he swayed, back and fro, he swayed
And how I listened and believed.

I remember my native land
   Although I walked away from it
   when I was only five.
   But that's a part of my life
Where I began.

I remember coming here, a different land,
   But I stood underneath the same sky
   And saw the same sun set and rise.
This was where I was to become. . . . And

I remember learning to speak again.
   How I came to understand

The difference in dialect of each land.
I began to accept changes.

I remember the happiness and pain
   of my yesterdays and todays.
   Again, I'll experience all that I've said
   and will say.
And—I don't regret walking on either stage.

I remember wanting to be older,
   thinking I would be set free
   from all I see.
And NOW I'm THERE, but where?

I remember how I came to realize,
   How I came to break my own chains
   And set free my fears and pain.
I came to know again the life
   that wore no disguise.

I remember unmasking,
   Believing once more in the fairy tales
   told by my father.
   And tasting the home cooking
   done by my mother.
That's when I gained my own being.

Carla Veiga
John D. O'Bryant High School

Excerpt from *Discovery: Award-Winning Writers in a Boston High School Competition.*

ACKERLEY

READING IS EVERYTHING ITS QWACKED UP TO BE

12.
Brown County Library

Green Bay, Wisconsin

Idea

Young adult summer reading program

Customers

Younger young adults, grades six through nine

Setting

Brown County Library, which includes a central facility, eight branches, and a bookmobile, serves a growing, predominantly Caucasian-American population of just under 200,000, of whom 6,383 are students in grades six through nine. Brown County is one of the fastest-growing counties in Wisconsin, with its minority population growing the fastest. It is a mix of urban and rural with a strong economy and low unemployment. Services to youth have been identified as one of the library's primary roles.

Program Description

The Choose Your Adventure YA Summer Reading Program was created in 1992 at the request of young teenagers who had participated in children's programs but wanted something that reflected their own interests. The program intended to

1. Create partnerships with businesses and agencies to offer reading incentives and opportunities for career exploration
2. Promote summer reading
3. Increase program involvement
4. Develop an end-of-summer event that acknowledged teen commitment to the reading program

Objectives included

1. Collaboration with twenty businesses
2. Four thousand books read
3. A 25 percent increase in teen participation
4. Attendance of 200 teens at the end-of-summer event

Rather than traditional prizes, readers were offered the chance to enter their name once for every 100 pages read in a drawing to win an "adventure" of their choice. Adventures donated by businesses and agencies included an airplane flyover with a chance at the controls and hosting a program on a radio station as a guest DJ. Young adult volunteers registered participants, recorded pages read, sorted adventure drawing slips, and tallied program statistics. In 1993 a teen survey was used to evaluate the program and gather suggestions for future projects.

Participation increased from 901 teens in 1991 (the baseline year before the program started) to 1,450 in 1992 and 1,317 in 1993; participating businesses grew from twenty in 1992 to twenty-seven in 1993; and attendance at the end-of-summer event rose from 240 to 275. Books read by YAs during the program years were 8,741 in 1992 and 10,158 in 1993.

Funding

The Green Bay Packers Foundation contributed $5,000 to overall summer reading programs. Of this donation, $1,000 was earmarked for the Choose Your Adventure program, to be used for entertainment, a pizza party, and publicity. Staff included a youth program coordinator, a YA librarian, and eight supporting staff plus a hundred YA volunteers.

Contact Person

Sue Wegge, Young Adult Librarian, Brown County Library, 515 Pine Street, Green Bay, WI 54301. (414) 448-4370

13.
Chicago Public Library, West Lawn Branch

Chicago, Illinois

Idea

Library-sponsored baseball team

Customers

Younger young adults, ages ten through fourteen

Setting

The program takes place in West Lawn, Chicago Lawn, and Gage Park Library communities, composed largely of Arab-American, Hispanic-American, African-American, and Eastern European populations, many of whom are first- generation immigrants coping with language and cultural barriers.

Program Description

The Blue Skies for Library Kids Baseball Team was sponsored in 1992 by the library as a way to provide organized activities neglected by neighborhood parks, collaborate with the Southwest Youth Services Baseball League, reach out to underserved teens, and improve the library's image in and contribution to the multicultural community.

Besides the fifteen to twenty young people on the library team, over fourteen young adults were involved as volunteers, coaches, and umpires, along with parents and community members. The library provided books in addition to trophies for team members, as well as a pizza and video party at the end of the season for players and their families. Books included age-appropriate fiction on baseball in 1992 and *The Guinness Book of Sports Records* in 1993. (The library team won three games in 1993 as opposed to none in 1992.)

Funding

The Blue Skies for Library Kids project is supported by a $1 million grant from the Chicago Community Trust through the Chicago Public Library Foundation. The grant supports projects in eighteen branches, of which this is one.

Contact Person

Barbara Basile, West Lawn Library, 4020 West 63rd Street, Chicago, IL 60629. (312) 747-7381

Blue Skies for Library Kids Baseball Team.

14.
Chicago Public Library, Hall and Robert Taylor Homes Branches

Chicago, Illinois

Idea

Summer job readiness training program

Customers

Younger young adults, ages thirteen through fifteen

Setting

This program is offered at the Hall and Robert Taylor Homes branches of the Chicago Public Library, located in the Grand Boulevard area of Chicago, the second poorest congressional district in the United States. This is an African-American community in which income is low, unemployment is high, crime is excessive, and housing is inadequate.

Program Description

The Job Readiness Program, a part of the Blue Skies for Library Kids project planned in re- sponse to a community needs assessment, trained twenty-eight and thirty young adults, respectively, during the summers of 1992 and 1993. The program involved eight-week training sessions on resume writing, interviewing, dressing for success, work behaviors, the application process, and other job-related skills. The participants also worked eight hours per week in the two library branches and made several field trips to various workplaces. The young adults were rewarded with a commencement ceremony and a $300 stipend.

The YA participants are now regular library users. Twenty are working on a mural with the Chicago Children's Museum, one has applied for a library page position, and one has decided on a future in work with computers.

Funding

The Blue Skies for Library Kids project is supported by a $1 million grant from the Chicago Community Trust through the Chicago Public Library Foundation. The grant supports projects in eighteen branches, of which this is one. The Robert Taylor Homes Boys and Girls Club paid the facilitators, arranged the field trips, and helped recruit participants.

Contact Person

Regina Johnson, Hall Branch Library, 4801 South Michigan Avenue, Chicago, IL 60615. (312) 747-2541

15.
District of Columbia Public Library and the School without Walls

Washington, D.C.

Idea

Equal exchange of information between students and librarians

Customers

At-risk, inner-city high school students

Setting

The program is offered at the Martin Luther King Memorial Library, the main library of the District of Columbia Public Library System in downtown Washington, D.C.

Program Description

Youth Exchange was established in January, 1993, to generate enthusiasm for reading among D.C. teens and to create lifelong library users and advocates. The twenty to twenty-five participants commit to reading a book every week, sharing their opinions orally in discussions at the MLK Library every Wednesday, filling out a written evaluation of each book, and learning how to prepare and present a booktalk to a class of their peers. In return, the young adults receive "service learning" credit from the School without Walls, an alternative high school within the public school system. Their advice is used by two professional librarians on the District of Columbia Public Library staff who serve on the ALA/YALSA Best Books for Young Adults Committee and also work toward improved YA collection development in the public library. In their school, the students maintain a log of summaries and critiques of each book read for use in creating a summer reading list and a schoolwide "literary trivia" activity in the fall.

Before each discussion, the young adults get a specially arranged behind-the-scenes library tour, are introduced to traditional and state-of-the-art reference tools and resources, and preview newly released YA films and videos to recommend whether they should be added to the collection.

Funding

Regular public library and public school budgets

Contact Person

Billie K. White, District of Columbia Public Library, 901 G Street, NW, Room 109, Washington, D.C. 20001. (202) 727-1295

Students participating in the reading program. Left to right: Rebecca Lemos, Angie Harper, Christina Pantoja, Jada Wells, D'Wanna Lee, Loren Becker, Mel Wingate-Bey, Tameka Campbell, Maggie Filardo.

16.
Edmond Memorial High School Library

Edmond, Oklahoma

Idea

Cooperative networking to promote student success in research

Customers

High school students, grades ten through twelve

Setting

The Edmond High School Library Media Center serves 1,740 students, who are mostly Caucasian-American from professional families in grades ten through twelve, in seven thousand square feet of space that houses fifteen thousand volumes, six hundred audiovisual and ninety-four periodical titles, an extensive vertical file, a small professional library for faculty, and a Career Center for counselors and students. The school is one of three high schools in a nineteen-school district serving over fifteen thousand students.

Program Description

Believing that early and consistently successful searching is the best predictor of students' desire to do future research and to become lifelong learners, the Edmond Memorial High School Library Media Center (EMHS) Network is linked internally within the high school and externally in the community to meet student information needs and promote success. EMHS is networked from the library to classrooms, where computers access the EMHS electronic catalog and CD-ROM files that include *Magazine Article Summaries* (noting other locations if the magazine is not owned by EMHS), full-text *Newsbank, Facts on File,* and *Social Issue Resource Series* (*SIRS*). EMHS library media specialists have prepared search tools and teach their usage to students and teachers. Class visits in the library are cooperatively planned in developing assignments. Both the science and social studies classes use the media center more because of classroom access to the network.

As part of MetroNetwork in the Oklahoma City area, which the EMHS library media specialist helped organize, participating libraries have access to an electronic bulletin board for help with reference questions, as well as fax machines for prompt response to magazine and ILL requests. EMHS is also a member of the Oklahoma Library Technology Network (OLTN) that the EMHS librarian helped form. The network provides access to the cataloging records of over 550 libraries for interlibrary loan through a dedicated work station in the media center that was loaned to EMHS by the state.

The career center includes the scholarship computer search programs Tuition Funding Strategies and OSU Finds as well as College and Career Search, plus the usual print test-preparation books, college directories, catalogs, and specific career information.

Circulation statistics indicated a 10 percent increase in October 1993 over the same period in 1992. Magazine requests are filled within twenty-four hours; ILL books usually within forty-eight.

Besides networking through technology, EMHS has also organized a monthly Drop Everything and Read (D.E.A.R.) period, during which everyone in the school stops and reads for pleasure, as well as a Great Books discussion program.

Funding

EMHS has an annual budget of $18,000, half of which is dedicated to standing orders, plus an average of $3,000 from photocopy and fine money. The $40 membership in the Oklahoma Union List of Serials is paid from the media center budget. The MetroNetwork dues (under $100) are paid by the school district for all its library media centers.

Contact Person

Bettie Estes-Rickner, Educational Services Coordinator, Edmond Public Schools, 215 North Boulevard, Edmond, OK 73034. (405) 340-2916

17.
Fort Bend County Libraries

Richmond, Texas

Piper Cub scale model airplane built by high school student, Paul Belik, for Fort Bend County Libraries.

Idea

A communitywide web of information services, materials, programs, cooperation, and networking for the benefit of young adults, with the public libraries as the unifying center

Customers

Young adults, ages twelve through eighteen

Setting

Fort Bend County's libraries serve a diverse population of more than 248,000 residents in one of the nation's fastest growing counties, which borders Houston and represents a volatile urban, suburban, and rural mix. Fort Bend County is the most ethnically diverse county in Texas and the eighth most diverse in the country. The George Memorial Library is the central library; there are two regional and two smaller branches and a mini-branch. Two new branches are in the planning stage.

Program Description

Community Partnership for Young Adults targets 25,282 youth in Fort Bend County with multiple library activities, including separate YA collections and areas; a "Sorry, We Tried" letter for students who have made an effort but cannot find needed information; book lists of different genres; an annotated list of Texas Lonestar Books with multiple copies attractively displayed; an amphitheater for pep rallies; school spirit displays, art and science exhibits, and performances; volunteer opportunities (ninety-five YAs and more than 1,500 hours in 1992); and unrestricted, free service seven days and four nights a week.

Partnership with schools includes: assignment alert forms for teachers; special teacher library cards; teacher orientations and information packets; a Library-School Advisory Task Force; homework centers with borrowed textbooks from area schools; library visits from teen-parent and child-care classes; extra credit for students volunteering to help with children's programs; Job Training Partnership Act (JTPA) workers; FBCL database accessible via computer and modem to all county schools; 65,000 library hours bookmarks distributed annually; YAs bused to library during the school day for orientation, tours, and help with assignments; and sharing school books and computers in the public library during the summer.

Partnership with the community features a $23,000 donated Science Center with books; an electronic encyclopedia; Apple and IBM hardware with twenty-five science programs and hands-on science exhibits (including a scale-model airplane with a five-foot wingspan made by a YA); support for multicultural programs, such as an Hispanic-American Arts festival; and programs on career choices and college scholarships, as well as program speakers, free consultants, and referral services.

Partnership with community agencies includes librarians certified as Red Cross baby-sitting instructors, the Fort Bend Community Information Service (FBCIS) list of community services accessible through the Library's Dynix system, and collaboration with the Fort Bend Family Health Center to promote services and programs for youth at risk.

Funding

The regular library budget, except for the Science Center

Contact Person

Molly Krukewitt, Coordinator of Youth Services, George Memorial Library, Fort Bend County Libraries, 1001 Golfview Drive, Richmond, TX 77469-5199. (713) 341-2634

18.
Iberia Parish Library

New Iberia, Louisiana

Idea

Summer educational hands-on workshops

Customers

Young adults, ages twelve through seventeen

Setting

This is a parishwide public library system consisting of a main library located in New Iberia's Civic Center and six branches. Together, they serve sixty-nine thousand residents, of whom sixty-seven hundred are young adults, ages twelve through seventeen. Iberia Parish has a depressed economy and supports no public museums, art galleries, or colleges. The parish is 68 percent Caucasian-American, many of whom are French and Acadian; 29 percent African-American; and 13 percent combined Hispanic-American, Asian-American, and Native American.

Program Description

Passport to Excitement and Adventure—Summer Workshops was begun eleven years ago to fill a perceived void in the library's summer activities for youth, which lacked appeal for those over age ten. The workshops are designed for all school-age children, free of charge, but

In model rocketry, students assemble their own Viking II rockets and hear a lecture by an astronomer from the local planetarium.

young adults, ages twelve through seventeen, are the primary target.

Workshops cover a wide variety of subjects, such as weaving, camping, fitness, bread making, agam painting, natural science, model rocketry, shopping, and fly tying. Most are held at the Main Library, some at appropriate alternate sites; several are field trips. A workshop leader and library staff design sessions to provide interactive, hands-on, educationally valid activities. At the end of each session, participants are given bookmark bibliographies on the topic, and these have an immediate effect on circulation of the listed materials. After a week-long registration in early May, a random drawing determines placement and notification of participants, since the free workshops are almost universally oversubscribed. Each person attends two workshops and can be an alternate for five more. At summer's end, each participant is mailed an evaluation form on which they can also suggest future programs.

In 1993 a total of 1,133 people applied for the seventy-four workshops. All were filled and had long lists of alternates. Ninety-four percent of participants rated their workshops either excellent or good. YAs over the 17-year-old maximum age have begun returning to assist with workshops, usually their favorites from previous years.

Funding

For eleven years funding has come from the Optimist Club of New Iberia, which provided $4,200 in 1993. The Optimist Club has also assisted staff in chaperoning field trips, scrounging supplies, and planning and executing specific workshops. The library provides two full-time staff members, and the Friends of the Library have provided $900 for an additional part-time person to administer the program. Almost every other staff member at the Main Library helps in some capacity. A community support system of parents, business owners, workshop leaders, and the media donates time, ideas, and goods. (For example, when the library needed fish for fish printing, people began dropping frozen fish at the circulation desk.)

Contact Person

Susan Hester Edmunds, Program Coordinator, Iberia Parish Library, 445 East Main Street, New Iberia, LA 70560. (318) 373-0075

19.
Meriden Public Library

Meriden, Connecticut

Idea

Summer computer literacy camp in the library

Customers

At-risk young adults, ages fourteen through twenty-one

Setting

Meriden Public Library is in downtown Meriden, an urban, diverse, working class city. Attendance at the library's youth services department averages 275 children a week from age six through adolescence, drawing an additional 150+ above average attendance at ten weekly story hours for special events. Outreach activities have included an annual Puerto Rican Family Festival, school Read-Alouds, classroom visits, and presentations at parent-teacher meetings.

Program Description

To provide meaningful summer activity to inner-city youth, the library provided a Summer On-Site Computer Camp during 1993. Approximately 75 young adults, recruited by the Meriden Community Action Agency from over 300 applicants to meet strict eligibility standards, learned computer literacy and job preparation skills on twelve leased Macintosh computers. The participants were also exposed to the library's adult computer center, which houses six additional personal computers. Classes were held eight times a week in the library; at other times, the young adults worked in various other city departments. Participants were encouraged to return during open hours to practice what they had learned in computer class.

Students who were unwilling at first became excited at what they could do and would work through break periods to do "just one more thing." Antisocial behavior diminished, and a small number of the target young adults have continued to be both library and computer users.

Funding

The program was funded by a state block grant under the Summer Work Employment and Education Program through the Meriden Community Action Agency. This grant provided for three computer teachers, three aides, and leasing of twelve personal computers. A second grant from Gov. Lowell Weicker's fund paid for the software used.

Contact Person

Kathie Matsil, Director of Youth Services, Meriden Public Library, Box 868, Meriden, CT 06450. (203) 238-2344, ext. 14

Meriden Public Library Summer Computer Camp: Denise Bell, Lakisha Brackett, and her sister Carlotta make use of computers available in the Children's Library.
(Photo by Chris Angileri, *Record Journal*, Meriden Connecticut.)

20.
Monroe County Public Library

Bloomington, Indiana

Idea

Drop-in math homework help

Customers

Secondary school students

Setting

Monroe County Library is a medium-sized library serving a county population of 108,978 (94.4 percent Caucasian-American), of whom 6,125 teens were enrolled in six public secondary schools in 1992. The area's economy is service-based and focused on Indiana University. There is no large city within fifty miles. A young-adult librarian, hired in 1989 to serve young adults, ages thirteen through twenty, organized ninety-eight programs and made eighty classroom presentations in 1992 to a combined audience of 4,216 young adults.

Program Description

Math Homework Help was started in 1989 in response to a YA survey that asked, "If the library could provide help with homework, what subject should it be?" To this question, 90 percent replied, "math." The program provides a social, out-of-school environment in which students can get help at prescheduled weekly times during the school year from volunteer tutors in the library. It is an intergenerational program that offers positive interactions between adults and teens and provides an opportunity for teens to know articulate adults who use math as an integral part of their careers.

Help is provided on a first-come, first-served basis from 7:00 to 9:00 P.M. each Monday evening. Attendance averages 11 to 18 per night (350 to 557 annually). Ten to fifteen tutors volunteer for the year, with four to eight working each Monday night. Tutors include local teachers, students, Indiana University faculty, engineers from a nearby naval weapons center, and teens themselves. Evaluation is based on statistics on attendance, math level, and school attended, and on occasional anecdotal comments used to evaluate student, tutor, and sponsor satisfaction.

Funding

Funding of $900 for tutor coordination is shared by three of the project's partners: the library, the local teachers union, and one of the county school corporations. Three other partners provide in-kind assistance and additional funds. The largest number of tutors are engineers from the NSWC Crane School Partnership Program; the Bloomington Chamber of Commerce helps to promote the program to its membership and has assisted in expanding it; and McDonald's Restaurant duplicated the program, hired a second tutor coordinator, and offers a Wednesday night session at the restaurant. All publicity flyers are produced by the McDonald's area representative.

Contact Person

Dana Burton, Youth Services Librarian, Monroe County Public Library, 303 East Kirkwood Avenue, Bloomington, IN 47408. (812) 339-2271

MATH HOMEWORK HELP
FREE, DROP-IN HELP FOR MIDDLE & HIGH SCHOOL STUDENTS

MONDAY NIGHTS 7-9 PM
Place: MONROE COUNTY PUBLIC LIBRARY
303 E. Kirkwood Ave., 3rd floor Staff room

WEDNESDAY NIGHTS 7-9 PM
Place: McDONALD'S WEST - 230 FRANKLIN ROAD
(Corner of Highway 37 & West 3rd Street)

What kind of help? Students will be helped on a drop-in, first come, first served basis. Tutors will be able to assist with:

ALGEBGRA ** GEOMETRY ** TRIGONOMETRY ** CALCULUS **
and BASIC MATH for SECONDARY STUDENTS

QUESTIONS: CALL 323-4349

This Partnership Project is funded and sponsored by:
Monroe County Education Association ** N.S.W.C. Crane School Partnership Program
Monroe County Public Library Youth Services ** McDonald's Restaurants

Flyer for Math Homework Help offered by the Monroe County Public Library.

21.
Richmond Public Schools and the Virginia Center for the Book

Richmond, Virginia

Idea

A meet-the-authors interactive teleconference with Virginia Hamilton and Arnold Adoff

Customers

Primarily middle school students; also some elementary, high school, and education students, teachers, school library media specialists, and public librarians

Setting

Richmond Public Schools, an urban school system with a multicultural enrollment, many of whom are disadvantaged and at risk, provided a live audience of two hundred students. Richmond was the first school system in Virginia to establish its own ITFS television station and studio to broadcast instructional programs to all its schools. Other interactive live sites within Virginia included Northside Middle School, Norfolk; the Learning Resource Center, James Madison University, and Harrisonburg Public Schools, Harrisonburg; and WBRA studios in Roanoke. The teleconference was also made available by satellite live to all middle and high schools in the state.

Program Description

Capitalizing on the Richmond site for Virginia Hamilton's Arbuthnot Honor Lecture, the Virginia Center for the Book and the Richmond Public Schools' Department of Media and Technology organized a statewide Meet-the-Authors Teleconference for her and her husband, author Arnold Adoff, the day after the lecture to provide a means for students all across Virginia to hear, see, and interact with two award-winning

authors. Extensive planning and publicity made sure that students were already familiar with the authors and their work and ready with questions. Marvin Curtis, who wrote his doctoral dissertation on Hamilton's *The People Could Fly*, worked with a group of Richmond students to videotape a choral reading of the story for broadcast before the teleconference as a special gift to the authors.

The program videotape is now available nationally through interlibrary loan from the Virginia State Library and Archives, from the Association for Library Service to Children (ALSC) at ALA, or by sending a blank videotape to the Virginia Center for the Book. As a result of this teleconference, the poet laureate Rita Dove has agreed to do a similar one in the spring of 1994.

Funding

The State Department of Information Technology was paid $1,200 to coordinate the satellite broadcast from the Virginia Center for the Book. Since the authors were already in Richmond for Virginia Hamilton's Arbuthnot Lecture the day before, they agreed to do the teleconference at no charge. Staff at Richmond Public Schools arranged student transportation and publicity; local school and public librarians handled local arrangements at other live sites; and two part-time Virginia Center for the Book staff members worked with staff from the Virginia State Library and Archives.

Contact Persons

Dr. Dolores Pretlow, Director, Media Technology, Richmond Public Schools, 301 North Ninth Street, Richmond, VA 23219. (804) 780-7693. Or Beverly Bagan, Executive Director, Virginia Center for the Book, Eleventh Street at Capitol Square, Richmond, VA 23219. (804) 371-6493

22.
Riverside City and County Public Library, Riverside Unified School District, and Alvord Unified School District

Riverside, California

Idea

Homework assistance centers; a Youth Advocacy Council to advise the library; library representation on citywide committees concerned with youth

Customers

At-risk middle school students

Setting

The homework assistance centers exist at two middle school sites and three RCCPL branches. Riverside's population is 26 percent Hispanic-American, 7.4 percent African-American, and 5.2 percent Asian-American; many of the last group speak English as a second language. The Riverside City and County Public Library is composed of twenty-nine branches throughout the County of Riverside.

Program Description

The collaborative Youth Outreach Program, designed in response to the Los Angeles riots that occurred only fifty miles away, is composed of three parts: five homework assistance centers (two in middle schools and three in public library branches), a YA library advisory board, and library representation on citywide committees implementing programs for youth or offering networking opportunities for youth services providers.

The homework assistance centers provide information access, assist with student literacy, increase self-esteem, and supply a technological connection between the school and public libraries. With the assis-

tance of forty high school and college tutors, middle schoolers may study, be tutored, use either library's outreach materials, work with computers and electronic encyclopedias, request public library materials, receive instruction in using the online public catalog, and have additional research assistance from 3:00 to 6:00 P.M. from two youth outreach librarians.

The Youth Advocacy Council helps plan YA programs, such as a recently sponsored fashion show; assists in video and book selection for young adults; and helped plan, design, and collate a recent youth survey that was distributed to every young person enrolled in the Riverside Unified School District.

The youth outreach librarians serve on the Librarians and Curriculum Councils of the school district, participate in school staff meetings at the middle school sites, and work with the citywide Child Advocacy Council, which is currently planning experiential learning job activities throughout the city.

Statistics for the first four months indicate that the homework centers were open 239 hours and answered sixteen questions per hour. Altogether, 1,515 students asked questions at the

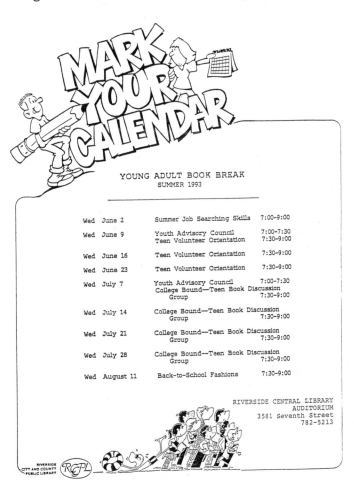

MARK YOUR CALENDAR

YOUNG ADULT BOOK BREAK
SUMMER 1993

Wed	June 2	Summer Job Searching Skills	7:00-9:00
Wed	June 9	Youth Advisory Council	7:00-7:30
		Teen Volunteer Orientation	7:30-9:00
Wed	June 16	Teen Volunteer Orientation	7:30-9:00
Wed	June 23	Teen Volunteer Orientation	7:30-9:00
Wed	July 7	Youth Advisory Council	7:00-7:30
		College Bound—Teen Book Discussion Group	7:30-9:00
Wed	July 14	College Bound—Teen Book Discussion Group	7:30-9:00
Wed	July 21	College Bound—Teen Book Discussion Group	7:30-9:00
Wed	July 28	College Bound—Teen Book Discussion Group	7:30-9:00
Wed	August 11	Back-to-School Fashions	7:30-9:00

RIVERSIDE CENTRAL LIBRARY
AUDITORIUM
3581 Seventh Street
782-5213

RIVERSIDE CITY AND COUNTY PUBLIC LIBRARY

centers, and 306 volunteer hours were given. Results from sign-in sheets show that young adults at the school sites would have no public library access without the centers. Three other middle and high schools are waiting to participate in the program.

Funding

Special funding was provided by the City Council of Riverside as a pilot for an LSCA grant. The pilot was considered so successful that it was replicated before filing an LSCA application. Funding covers two youth outreach librarians, one University of California at Riverside intern, and four part-time library pages.

Contact Persons

Nora Jane Natke, Youth Services Coordinator, Riverside City and County Public Library, 3021 Franklin Street, Riverside, CA 92507. (909) 369-3003, ext. 230. Or Jeane Beaird or Sandra Eckert, Youth Outreach Librarians, Central Library, 3581 Seventh Street, Riverside, CA 92502. (909) 782-5211

23.
South Kingston School Department

Wakefield, Rhode Island

Idea

Oral history project

Customers

Fifteen tenth graders

Setting

South Kingston High School is a suburban high school of 950 students with a modern media center, an English department of twelve teachers, and a varied and flexible curriculum. The school population is about 8 percent minority, including Native Americans, African-Americans, and foreign students whose parents may be connected with the University of Rhode Island.

Program Description

The Family in the Fifties: Hope, Fear, and Rock 'n Roll was a semester-long oral history project that culminated in a publication and two public forums. The publication will be distributed to all public and school libraries in Rhode Island. The public forums included one in the high school media center, focused on civil liberties, and one on popular culture at the Rhode Island Historical Society. A team consisting of librarian, teacher, and two historians from the University of Rhode Island worked with students to develop the historical, literary, and social themes of the postwar decade. They advised students on the questions to ask, how to ask them, and what to look for when writing the interviewees' stories. Selections of literature, poetry, and drama were used to illustrate a vari-

The Family in the Fifties

Hope, Fear & Rock 'n Roll

An Oral History of Rhode Island in the Post-War Decade

Written by Tenth Grade Students at South Kingstown High School

ety of themes. The school library media specialist brought to the classroom relevant media center resources in a variety of formats; recruited guest lecturers such as Chuck Stevens, a radio disc jockey from the fifties; and also coordinated the project with the scholars and with personnel at the Rhode Island Historical Society.

Funding

A $14,000 grant from the Rhode Island Committee on the Humanities included an outside evaluator; in-kind contributions drew upon the Rhode Island Historical Society's personnel and library resources

Contact Person

Linda P. Wood, School Library Media Specialist, South Kingston High School, 215 Columbia Street, Wakefield, RI 02879. (401) 792-9611

24.
Washington State Young Adult Review Group (WASHYARG)

Seattle, Washington

Idea

Regional librarian reviewing organization

Customers

School and public librarians and other individuals interested in materials appropriate for adolescent use and content

Setting

King County Library System Service Center in Seattle was the site of this program. Members represent the culturally diverse population of the Puget Sound area and western Washington and include a few Canadians, Alaskans, and Oregonians.

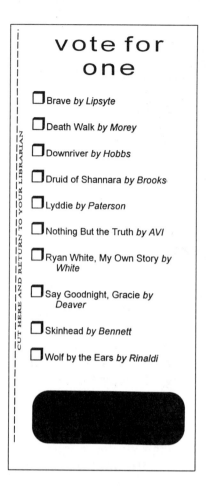

Program Description

The Washington State Young Adult Review Group (WASHYARG) is a twenty-year-old regional reviewing organization with the goal of reviewing all types of materials and raising awareness of young-adult literature, while helping school and public librarians responsible for young-adult collections to make informed choices in a timely and cost-effective way. This goal is met through quarterly review meetings; a quarterly publication of reviews called *The Washrag*; continuing education credits for those attending who wish them; provision of book lists, suggestions, conference sessions, and statewide networking on YA titles, trends, and intellectual freedom issues; and the annual Evergreen Award program for young-adult favorites.

Over 180 members actively participate, with 100 in attendance at a typical meeting led by a permanent and a rotating chair. Reviewers present starred fiction titles (often accompanied by vociferous audience remarks) for about an hour followed by a brief program. More reviews are followed by a brief business meeting, announcements, and a brown bag lunch, after which nonfiction is reviewed.

While there are only a few dues-paying YA members, ten King County Youth Advisory Groups do reviews, as do most of the school library classes. The Evergreen Award is based on YA-picked titles and votes.

Funding

The program is supported by annual dues, set at fifteen dollars per member as of 1993. (For nineteen years annual dues were five dollars.)

Contact Person

Susan B. Madden, King County Library System, 300 Eighth Avenue North, Seattle, WA 98109. (206) 684-6626

Education Support

25.
Austin Public Library

Austin, Texas

Idea

One-to-one volunteer tutoring and homework assistance

Customers

At-risk students grades one through twelve

Setting

The program is offered at branch library locations of Austin Public Library. In 1992–93 25.2 percent of Austin high school students dropped out of school. Nine of the Austin Independent School District's 100 schools (each with high numbers of low-income and minority students) may be closed within two years because 20 percent or fewer students passed all sections of the state's achievement test in the spring of 1993.

Program Description

The VICTORY (Volunteers in Communities Tutoring Our Responsible Youth) Program addresses the need of Austin's young people to continue their education, perform at grade level, and graduate. The program was organized in response to numerous requests from youth for tutoring at the library. In 1992 and 1993 229 young adults (grades six through twelve) were assisted by volunteer tutors once or twice a

Do You Need Help With Your Homework or Studying for Tests?

If the Answer is Yes, We Can Help.

CALVIN AND HOBBES copyright Watterson. Dist. by UNIVERSAL PRESS SYNDICATE. Reprinted with permission. All rights reserved.

The Austin Public Library's VICTORY Program is offering free tutoring to students in grades 1-12. Call any of the following Austin Public Library locations for more information.

Carver Branch
1161 Angelina
472-6832

Oak Springs Branch
3101 Oak Springs Drive
926-7219

Govalle Branch
4704-A East First Street
385-4825

Terrazas Branch
1105 East First Street
385-4825

Manchaca Road Branch
5500 Manchaca Road
447-6052

University Hills Branch
4721 Loyola Lane
929-3037

City of Austin

week. Tasks and goals are set by the student and tutor together, allowing the students individual control over the development of their own objectives and interests.

Student input is sought through interviews; parents and tutors participate through Advisory Council meetings and quarterly tutor meetings. Each branch manager is consulted quarterly to evaluate the program's achievements. To organize these efforts, the eight VISTA volunteers meet weekly, and once each month branch managers and Youth Services Division staff meet with the volunteers. The effectiveness of the program is analyzed with the assistance of a volunteer statistician. The tutoring program is augmented during the summer by enrichment programs in math and the improvement of reading skills. Eighty more young adults took advantage of these summer offerings.

Funding

One federally funded member of VISTA (Volunteers in Service to America) was assigned to each of the eight participating branches to coordinate tutor schedules. In-kind contributions included the work of the 250 volunteer tutors. Kraft Foods donated $2,500 and the East Austin Community Foundation gave $1,000. Nine sets of books worth $3,500 were provided by Steck-Vaughn, and there were multiple small grants and contributions from community sponsors.

Contact Person

Irma Flores-Manges, Manager, Youth Services Division, Austin Public Library, P.O. Box 2287, Austin, TX 78768. (512) 499-7325

♻ This section is recyclable   •   Thursday, March 12, 1992   Austin American-Statesman **B3**

Library seeks VISTA workers for tutoring program

By Mike Todd
American-Statesman Staff

Efforts to help failing students bring up their grades and stay in school would be expanded under a city library program.

The Austin Public Library is applying for five VISTA workers to coordinate tutoring at branch libraries. The workers would be paid by the federal government.

Lisa Miller-Gray, the city library's coordinator of volunteer services, said federal officials have been encouraging, and she believes the volunteers will be assigned to Austin if the City Council endorses the application Thursday.

Since beginning 12 years ago, tutoring at city libraries has expanded to the point where branch

> ❝We're at the point now where we need some help with on-site coordination.❞
>
> — Lisa Miller-Gray, library volunteer coordinator

librarians who have managed the programs need help, Miller-Gray said.

Last year, 104 tutors at four branch libraries donated more than 800 hours of service, she said. In the past three years, she said, the program has increased by 20 tutors a year.

"It's been a very viable program," Miller-Gray said. "It's been great and we've done well, but we're at the point now where we need some help with on-site

coordination."

VISTA, or Volunteers in Service to America, is the domestic version of the Peace Corps. Miller-Gray said VISTA workers would be stationed at Carver, Govalle, Oak Springs, Manchaca Road and University Hills branch libraries.

At public schools in those areas, 30 percent of the students perform below grade level, Miller-Gray said. The tutoring program's object is to reduce that number and keep students from dropping out.

Tutoring has helped, she said, and community support has been high.

Tau Beta Pi, the University of Texas service organization of honors engineering students, has provided 15 to 20 tutors a year for eight years, Miller-Gray said. Motorola and the Society of Black Engineers offers higher-math instruction two nights a week at University Hills, she said.

Miller-Gray said the library system should know within three months if the federal agency will provide the workers. The program would cost the city nothing, she said. The library system would be responsible for paying the workers' mileage, but Friends of the Austin Public Library has offered to cover that, she said.

26.
Lincoln City Libraries

Lincoln, Nebraska

Idea

Homework center

Customers

Middle and high school students, grades six through twelve

Setting

The program is offered at the Anderson Branch of the Lincoln City Libraries, a public library system serving a population of 214,000 (95 percent Caucasian-American) in Lincoln and Lancaster County, Nebraska. Anderson Branch serves one high school and three middle schools in a blue-collar neighborhood with a total of 3,750 students in grades six through twelve.

Program Description

The Homework Center at Anderson Branch Library provides a separate place within the branch for middle and senior high school students to call their own. The center was established in 1990 to meet an often stated but until then unmet need to provide an area for young adults. The collection includes approximately twelve hundred books, mostly age-appropriate leisure reading paperbacks, but also three encyclopedia sets for checkout and one CD-ROM *Grolier's Encyclopedia.* Use has been high, and circulation averages 4,500 items per year. A young-adult librarian position has been funded for Anderson Branch. This person's duties include coordinating the Homework Center with Lincoln Public Schools and other library activities in Lincoln. The young-adult librarian also sees that the Homework Center collection is supported by appropriate reference interview techniques and knowledgeable readers' advisory services, as well as acting as an advocate for this age group.

Funding

Regular library budget

Contact Person

Martha Brey MacCallum, Coordinator, Youth Services, Bennett Martin Public Library, 136 South Fourteenth Street, Lincoln, NE 68508. (402) 441-8565

Student working at the homework center.

Information Services

27.
Juneau Douglas High School Library

Juneau, Alaska

Idea

Multi-type library resource sharing

Customers

The program serves 1,400 high school students and 117 staff, including 73 teachers and 4 administrators.

Setting

This program is available through the Juneau Douglas High School Library. Douglas High School is the only high school in Juneau, and an average population of a thousand students, staff, and community members come to the library daily. The school district is 70.6 percent Caucasian-American, 19.7 percent Alaska Native and Native American, 5.6 percent Asian-American, 2.3 percent Hispanic-American, and 1.8 percent African-American.

Program Description

Capital City Libraries (CCL) is a unique multitype library cooperative. An entire community of twenty-five thousand shares resources and a patron database. A common library card secures use of collections in the one high school library, three public libraries, one university library, and the state libraries. Services include a com-

Multi-purpose library card.

bined online public access catalog (with dial-up access) of library holdings, direct loan to the public by all libraries, and daily interlibrary courier delivery. CCL embodies the Alaskan spirit—"Alaska is a Library!"—schools included! The JDHS Library joined CCL in July, 1988, believing that access for youth is important and that schools are valuable participants in resource sharing.

CCL goals are to

1. Provide the best possible services to citizens of Juneau of all ages through community-wide resource sharing
2. Optimize limited resources through resource sharing and cooperative collection development
3. Prepare students to become library and information literate

4. Meet the needs for access to information in a state capital
5. Maintain an automated circulation and on-line catalog that embodies the goals of communitywide resource sharing
6. Promote a multitype library system that uses one library card and provides direct loan to all patrons from member libraries

JDHS students and staff have come to rely on resources beyond their walls to teach, to do research, to complete assignments, and to read. Resource sharing is an institutionalized part of education at JDHS, with the library media center being a net CCL borrower. To purchase the 4,188 books borrowed from CCL libraries in 1992–93 would have cost the JDHS library over $100,000. Because of the ease of access to a wide variety of materials at all levels, students are more likely to succeed in class, and teachers are able to tailor units knowing that with a little advance planning a wealth of material can be used in the library or in their classrooms.

JDHS students use CCL at JDHS and at any of the other five libraries. The terminals and software are the same communitywide, with all librarians having a share in teaching youth. Dial-up to the catalog via modem is available so that students can use the catalog from home, place holds, and have materials delivered to the library of their choice. Students can also use WLNs Laser Cat to identify resources outside Juneau, which are then ordered.

Funding

The JDHS Library Media Center has a budget of $24,000. Capital equipment and software for CCL have cost the member libraries more than $900,000 since the project began in 1986. Since 1988, when JDHS joined, the school district's contribution for capital equipment has been $14,000. Funding came from a variety of sources—capital improvement funds from new library construction and JDHS's interlibrary co-

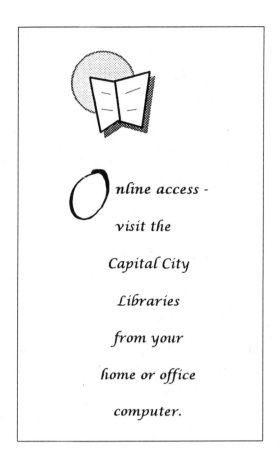

*O*nline access - visit the Capital City Libraries from your home or office computer.

operation grant. Each library used local funds for staffing to link records and for equipment. Local money is also used to fund ongoing maintenance of the system, training, and courier services. Costs per year for JDHS are slightly over $6,000 paid from district funds ($4,500 administration and $1,600 courier service). Each library pays a share of system administration computed on a formula based on the number of titles, terminals and circulation, although the state library hires the system administrator. Courier service is contracted by the university.

Contact Person

Ann K. Symons, Librarian, Juneau Douglas High School Library, Juneau School District, 10014 Crazy Horse Drive, Juneau, AK 99801. (907) 463-1947

28.
King County Library System

Seattle, Washington

Idea

Library within juvenile detention facility

Customers

At-risk detained youth, ages ten through seventeen, many of whom are illiterate, poor or reluctant readers, non–English speakers or readers, or unfamiliar with libraries. Offenses range from traffic violations to property crimes and serious felonies. In the past three years, the percentage of youth charged with violent crimes such as assault, armed robbery, sex offenses, or murder has risen dramatically, as has the recidivism rate.

Setting

The Youth Service Center is the juvenile detention facility for King County, Washington, located in Seattle. The present facility, which opened in January, 1993, houses up to 150 accused and adjudicated youth, ages ten through seventeen, who are held in detention for an average stay of ten days. Some youth awaiting trial for serious offenses are detained for up to eight months or longer. The center includes a school program operated by Seattle Public Schools; chaplaincy, recreation, drug, and alcohol programs; a health clinic; and the library.

Program Description

The Youth Service Center Library is an institutional branch of the King County Library System that serves the county juvenile detention facility. The goal of the YSC Library program is to meet the library needs of detained youth by making recreational, educational, informational, and cultural materials available to both residents and staff. The library is open seven days a week. Each living hall has its own regularly scheduled fifty-minute library period three times a week. Accompanied by a juvenile supervisory officer, the residents visit in groups of twelve or fewer.

Attempting to engage youth in activities that capitalize on their interests and also to encourage them to view libraries as resources wherever they live, the library provides a wide range of formats: music cassettes, magazines, books, posters, crafts, comics, stickers, newspapers, games, programs, rubber stamps, catalogs, puzzles, bulletin boards, and pamphlets. There is also a staff library and online access to the more than forty King County libraries.

A tremendously popular activity center, the YSC Library is a congenial, well-lit space where young people reflect, read, listen to music, or converse. Detainees and staff alike look forward to library time and use the wide-ranging collection extensively. The collection includes Spanish-language books, reading materials in Vietnamese, and large Native American and African-American studies collections, as well as vocational and career information, a reference section, materials on drug and alcohol issues and sexuality (including contraception, pregnancy, abortion, sexual orientation, and AIDS information). Other popular areas are poetry, drawing and art books, jokes and humor, and horror and science fiction. Residents also have access to the complete holdings of the King County Library system.

Library staff members are constantly reminded of the effect of the library by announcements such as "I never went to a library before detention." Or "That was a great book! Do you have another just like it?" Or "I only read when I'm here." Or "I started reading when I came to detention."

Funding

The YSC Library is supported through an annual contract between King County and the King County Library System, which totals $122,250 in 1994 ($99,750 for personnel, $2,500 for administrative overhead, and $20,000 for materials). Staff includes two three-quarter-time M.L.S. librarians and one half-time library assistant.

Contact Persons

Andrea Avni or Jill Morrison, Youth Service Center Library, 1211 East Alder, Seattle, WA 98122. (206) 343-2641 (after 10:00 A.M., Pacific time, Monday through Friday)

29.
Muscatine Community School District

Muscatine, Iowa

Idea

Electronic information network

Customers

Seventeen hundred high school students, grades nine through twelve

Setting

Muscatine High School is the only high school in Muscatine, Iowa, a city of twenty-four thousand that also has nine elementary and two middle schools plus a community college. The high school population is 14 percent Hispanic-American, and 34.6 percent of the students receive free or reduced-price lunches. Sixty percent of the high school's graduates go on to two- or four-year colleges.

Program Description

The Information Access Network (IAN) has been operational since September, 1993. The IAN consists of twenty-four IBM workstations in the media center networked with an identical number in the language arts department by an IBM PS/2 Server 195 and a smaller server (PS/2 Server 85) controlling a fourteen-drive CD-ROM tower. Four Macintosh workstations provide graphics scanning and desktop publishing capabilities. Software applications include *Facts on File, INFOTRAC, Grolier's Multimedia Encyclopedia, Choices, SIRS,* and an online library catalog. Objectives of the IAN are to

1. Provide students with electronic search technology to locate information accurately and efficiently
2. Help students gain a better understanding of what research is, how to connect knowledge, and how to refine topics
3. Expose teachers to new styles of teaching utilizing technology
4. Provide an introduction to word processing, allowing students to produce a finished product electronically
5. Develop computer skills for lifelong learning

The IAN hours of operation are 7:30 A.M. to 3:30 P.M., plus evening hours begun second semester for additional service (open until 8:00 P.M. each Thursday). Faculty become involved as their students use the system; advanced students utilize sophisticated search strategies, while at-risk and learning-disabled students no longer struggle to use an index or card file, resulting in a big decrease in frustration. The IAN involves traditional nonusers of the media center because it has many offerings available to departments such as math and industrial arts in addition to customary patrons such as language arts and social studies departments. Students from other buildings, as well as visitors from outside the district, come here to utilize the system and become aware of its potential and power.

The electronic information search helps develop thinking as students come across a variety of perspectives on a topic and realize that problems can be solved in different ways. Students are forced to decide which steps to take; to evaluate the information they access in terms of relevance, authority, and credibility; and to manipulate that information to solve a problem or express an idea with more time to edit, clarify, and evaluate the information because the drudgery of manual searching has been eliminated. Students' chances for success are also enhanced because of familiarity with workplace technology.

Funding

A $215,859 grant from the Roy J. Carver Charitable Trust was received in January 1993. IAN is under the direction of two professional media specialists with limited assistance from two clerical aides who also perform other library duties.

Contact Person

Becky Mather, Media Specialist, Muscatine High School, 2705 Cedar Street, Muscatine, IA 52761. (319) 263-6141, ext. 161

Programs and Services

30.
Cuyahoga County Public Library

Cleveland, Ohio

Idea

Information kits for loan to young adults in residential institutions

Customers

Approximately four thousand at-risk institutionalized teenagers who have no access to traditional library service

Setting

The kits are available to residential institutions such as homeless shelters, runaway shelters, rehabilitation clinics, correctional facilities, and hospitals in Cuyahoga County, Ohio.

Program Description

Leap Ahead is the Cuyahoga County Public Library (CCPL) outreach project designed to offer traditional library services and programs to informationally disadvantaged young adults who spend part or all of their adolescence in residential institutions. The project's primary objective is to make fifty subject-related kits, filled with a cross-section of library materials and activity ideas, available for a three-week loan to institutions housing adolescents, thus creating a bridge between the agencies, the at-risk teens

who live in them, and the public library. The materials in each Leap Ahead kit take into consideration a variety of reading levels as well as different cultures and cultural issues. The materials are intended to help young adults become informed and productive members of the communities in which they live and to make them think of the library as a vital part of that community upon deinstitutionalization.

Leap Ahead kit materials were selected by the project coordinator and a small committee of young adult services staff. Because so many YA staff are part-time, it is difficult to plan and execute regionwide or systemwide projects. Leap Ahead was a premiere opportunity for this to be accomplished by inviting interested staff to purchase materials and write activity ideas.

Leap Ahead also offered an opportunity to build relationships with youth-serving agencies. An advisory panel was formed in the planning stages of the project and met regularly at various sites around Cuyahoga County to gain input on the subjects to be included. Members also took ideas back to the youth in their institutions for end-user feedback. Teenagers in the institutions also met directly with the advisory panel to discuss information for which they felt a critical need: AIDS, black issues, parenting, sexuality, conflict resolution, and violence, among others. The advisory panel still maintains contact through Leap Ahead programs and publicity.

At the end of Leap Ahead's first year, every user and potential user was mailed an evaluation form that tried to ascertain whether he or she had heard about the project or used a kit and whether the kit met its objectives of being accessible to both staff and students. The return rate (approximately 75 percent) was encouraging and helped the library identify several new groups of potential users, such as neighborhood centers with teen programs and teens in treatment centers for the behaviorally handicapped. Evaluation is ongoing as CCPL's AV and Booking Service Department restocks each kit with an evaluation card.

Funding

An LSCA Title I grant of $12,000 provided start-up funding. The maintenance cost of $2,000 a year, needed to refurbish old kits and gradually add new ones, is met by CCPL. Materials selection and drafting of activity ideas consumed three months of professional time.

Contact Person

Cynthia Glunt, Regional Young Adult Services Manager, Mayfield Regional Branch, Cuyahoga County Public Library, 6080 Wilson Mills Road, Cleveland, OH 44143. (216) 473-0350

LEAP AHEAD
The Library's Project for Teens

Comments about this exciting new service...
"Excellent!...videos were exceptionally well done."
"The kids were actually inspired to read..."
"[Our teens] were enthused and highly motivated."
"You have truly filled a need for programming in this institution."

Kits of subject related materials are available for you to borrow and use for three weeks. Each kit contains books, videocassettes, audiocassettes, posters, games, activity ideas, pamphlets, and booklists. Great for use in small or large groups.

Some Subjects Currently Available

Aids	**Just for Fun**
Parenting	**More Fiction**
Personal Issues	**More Fun**
College Preparation	**Multicultural**
Conflict Resolution	**Relationships**
Current Issues: Environment	**School Days**
Current Issues: Violence	**Self Esteem I & II**
Easy Fiction	**Sexuality**
Express Yourself	**Sports I & II**
Fiction	**Substance Abuse**
Inside/Outside	**Surviving Adolescence**
	Teen Issues

To reserve these materials, **call Audio Visual Booking Services at 398-4404, weekdays, 8 a.m. to 5 p.m.,** for pick up at the Cuyahoga County Public Library near you. You will need a Cuyahoga County Public Library card. For more information, call 473-0350.

Cuyahoga County Public Library.
It's more than you think.

■

YOUNG ADULT SERVICES

31.
Langston Hughes Middle School, Fairfax County Public Schools

Reston, Virginia

Idea

Multicultural writers in residence

Customers

Middle school students, grades seven and eight

Setting

The program is offered at the Langston Hughes Middle School, part of the Fairfax County Public Schools system in the Virginia suburbs of Washington, D.C. Formerly an intermediate school, the large middle school only has the two grades. The student population is 58 percent Caucasian-American, 19 percent African-American, 13 percent Hispanic-American, 10 percent Asian-American, and two students are Native American. Unique services at the school include centers for English as a second language (ESL), gifted and talented and disabled students, and an art honors class, as well as peer helping, mediation, and mentoring programs.

Program Description

Building upon an authors-in-residence program begun in 1983, the first of its kind in the Fairfax County Public Schools district, the two-year-old Multicultural Authors-in-Residence program spans the curriculum. The middle school hosts writers during special events such as Virginia Reading Month and School Library Media Month. Writers are selected based on their literary achievements and experience in working with young people in an educational setting. The writers are then invited to present a workshop on writing and publishing as part of the regular school program. Objectives of the program are to

1. Reinforce the language arts curriculum's emphasis on the writing process
2. Enhance the self-concept and self-esteem of students
3. Meet the needs of the diverse student body with role models for students
4. Improve the academic achievement and aspirations of underachievers and minority students

Writers who have appeared include Eloise Greenfield, Sharon Bell Mathis, Paula Underwood Spencer, Walter Dean Myers, Ernest Gaines, Augusta Baker, Jan Spivey Gilchrist, Pinkie Gordon Lane, and Cheryl and Wade Hudson.

The day in residence includes workshops, student assemblies, and individual classroom sessions. Students, who are encouraged to read the author's works before the day in residence or to whom the library media specialist has read parts of the books, are thrilled to meet the authors of their books and ask for autographs, treating the authors like celebrities. Some reluctant readers are inspired to read after they have met the author, and books by an author in residence circulate constantly after the visit. Besides the students, LHMS faculty, staff, parents, and media center volunteers, representatives of other public schools, members of the community, and public librarians are also invited to the program, often for special workshops such as one on motivating reluctant readers by Walter Dean Myers or another on storytelling by Augusta Baker. Evaluation involves written feedback by both teachers and students, not only on the popularity and usefulness of the presentation, but also on what they learned about the author's writing process. Students are also asked to produce original writing based on the style and/or techniques of the particular writer.

Funding

A grant ($1,175 in 1992–93) from Fairfax County Public Schools is supplemented, if needed, by the Langston Hughes Middle School principal.

Contact Person

Diane E. Guilford, Langston Hughes Middle School, 11401 Ridge Heights Road, Reston, VA 22091. (703) 715-3652

AUTHORS IN RESIDENCE...

The **Hughes Authors in Residence Program** began in 1983. Head Librarian Diane Guilford started the program inviting authors to share their writing experiences with Hughes students. When Sharon Bell Mathis shared her creative writing experiences, she involved students in her presentation. This tradition of creative writing students participating in these school assemblies is still being featured in the program.

A special **Minority Author in Residence Grant** enhanced the program this year. The authors who visit under this grant will serve as role models for all Hughes students, especially the minority students.

Walter Dean Myers highlighted the Authors in Residence Program with an informal presentation for students and a workshop for faculty on motivating the reluctant reader. Other Fairfax County school personnel were invited to attend the workshop which may be presented on cable television.

32.
Mesa Public Library

Mesa, Arizona

Idea

General young adult services program

Customers

Young adults, ages twelve through eighteen or those in grades seven through twelve and others outside that age range who are interested

Setting

The Mesa Public Library consists of a large central library and two neighborhood branches, which serve a population of three hundred thousand, of whom approximately 10 percent are young adults (10.9 percent Hispanic-American, 1.9 percent African-American, 1.5 percent Asian-American, and 1 percent Native American). The library board, appointed by the mayor and city council, includes two young adults, one a voting member and one a Young Adult Advisory Council representative. Of the 599,500 items in the library's collection, approximately 11 percent are for young adults, and YA materials also accounted for 11 percent of the total circulation of 2,235,230 during the 1992–93 fiscal year. The branches have YA collections, but only the central library has a staffed, separate room for teens.

Program Description

Mesa Public Library's Young Adult Services is the only self-contained, fully staffed YA department in Arizona. It was established in 1976 by an LSCA grant to aid the adolescent individual in making a successful transition from the children's room to the adult room by providing

1. Programs and services that encourage use of the library by young adults
2. High-interest materials that support reading for recreational and personal enrichment
3. Materials, services, and programs that support self-awareness and personal development among young adults

4. Teachers, youth counselors, parents, and others who deal with teenagers with information to help them interact with the young adult age group
5. A staff skilled in working with young adults and their library needs

The program also fosters the continued use and support of the library by youth into adulthood. The Young Adult Department manages a young adult room that is situated appropriately between the children's and adult sections and features a painted mural representing subjects contained in this specialized department. Patrons may use the board game collection or listen to noncirculating CDs with headphones and players. Mesa's Youth Placement Service also maintains a job bulletin board for local teens.

The Young Adult Department also sponsors a Young Adult Advisory Council (YAAC) that meets twice monthly to review books and films. More than twenty-five teenagers served on this committee in 1992. Many former members still visit to report on what they are doing now and ask about past members. One alumnus noted, "I had many a good friend here and good librarians. Growing up with the Mesa Public Library meant a lot to me, and I will remember it fondly." YAAC members are considered official library volunteers and help at community events as well as with library programs. The YA Department also maintains a separate volunteer staff that assists with games, CDs, and headphones for the listening center; answers simple directional questions; and performs a variety of other tasks. In addition to YAAC members and volunteers, community service workers and youth service organizations provide extra help. During 1992–93, volunteers gave 2,305 hours.

School visits are vital in reaching Mesa's student population. YA staff introduce the public library with booktalks or storytelling, departmentally produced bibliographies, and a brochure listing crisis telephone numbers. As an alternative to on-site school visits, YA has also videotaped booktalks that are available through the schools' central media services. Near the end of the school year, the YA staff visit most of the sixth graders, inviting them to become involved at the library. Tours are also available. In 1992 the YA staff saw more than 5,650 students at the schools.

Programming is an important outreach tool,

For the first time at Mesa Public Library!

Cheap Thrills

Summer Reading
for ages 12-18
(grades 7-12)

▶ Earn coupons for free things to eat and do!

▶ Chances to win weekly drawings!

▶ A chance at the Grand Prize! A CD/Cassette Player!

Registration begins June 5!

Main Library
64 E. 1st St.
644-2734

Dobson Ranch Branch
2425 S. Dobson Rd.
644-3441

and the library's YAAC and volunteers give the department input on relevant concerns and interests. YA has a number of ongoing programs to entice YAs into the library—a chess club, Pen-Pals, and *E.T.*, a science fiction and fantasy magazine produced by local junior and senior high school students. YA has held workshops on babysitting, calligraphy, cartooning, creative writing, how to get published, sign language, and science fiction and fantasy illustration; helped new seventh graders address "junior high jitters"; hosted visiting authors; set up a medieval weapons demonstration; and sponsored programs on preparing for the SAT and finding money for college. In 1993, YA sponsored its first teen summer reading program, called Cheap Thrills. Assisted mainly by YA volunteers, 788 young adults participated. In 1994 YA hopes to expand the program to include junior high school sites.

Circulation plays a major role in the evaluation of Young Adult Services. It increased from 94,240 items in 1983 to 168,200 in 1992. Usage statistics are compiled semiannually during Typical Week periods, and YA is currently assessing a random survey of area junior and senior high schools.

Funding

Nine percent of the total library budget funds young adult initiatives, including materials and a staff of three—two professionals and a library associate. All programming is funded by the Friends of the Mesa Public Library. There are one full-time YA supervisory librarian, two part-time YA librarians, one full-time YA library associate, and a clerk to assist with summer activities.

Contact Persons

Diane Tuccillo, Young Adult Department, or Kate Havris, Reference Department, Mesa Public Library, 64 East First Street, Mesa, AZ 85201-6768. (602) 644-2735

33.
Miami-Dade Public Library System

Miami, Florida

Idea

Annual Black History Month community outreach program

Customers

African-American young adults, ages twelve through eighteen

Setting

The program is offered at North Dade Regional Library of the Miami-Dade Public Library System, located in a predominantly African-American community of whom 12.6 percent are young adults ages twelve through eighteen. Although there is a nearby enclave of expensive homes owned by African-Americans, the library's service area is mostly middle class with many single-family homes, some apartment buildings, and several low-income housing projects.

Program Description

The Black Leaders of the 90's Symposium consists of an evening at the library, where area families are invited to listen to African-American role models speak about how they transcended the disadvantages of their youth and became successful members of society. The annual symposium has taken place each February in conjunction with other Black History Month activities since 1990. The program encourages African-American youth to look beyond stereotypical images of the black community and see what possibilities lie before them. Additional goals include

1. Promoting an awareness of library resources and capabilities to African-American community leaders
2. Attracting African-American youth to the library for a social experience rather than a research experience
3. Showcasing the North Dade Regional Library's extensive African-American collection. Featured speakers are African-American judges, police officers, writers, community activists, doctors, lawyers, architects, and religious leaders.

All staff members are invited to provide input for a talent pool of potential speakers, who are then contacted. Besides publicity in the library system's quarterly program guide, posters and flyers, and press releases to local media, library staff visit area junior and senior high schools to develop interest in the program. The program itself lasts about an hour, with each speaker given ten to fifteen minutes. Presenters may choose to tell about their personal or professional lives. Usually, serious speakers are followed by the less serious to keep momentum going. Presentations are followed by a question-and-answer period and refreshments, when the young adults can interact with the speakers informally.

Attendance has fluctuated. In 1990 70 youth and 100 adults attended; in 1991 140 youth but fewer adults; in 1992 and 1993 there was a slight drop in attendance. In 1994 the symposium was conducted in conjunction with the library system's systemwide black history celebration, which included art exhibits and live entertainment.

Funding

Regular library budget. Presenters donate their time.

Contact Person

Raette King-Kee, Young Adult Librarian, North Dade Regional Library, 2455 NW 183rd Street, Miami, FL 33056. (305) 625-6424

34.
New York Public Library, St. George Library Center

Staten Island, New York

Idea

Electronic youth sign board

Customers

All young adults, ages twelve through eighteen or grades seven through twelve

Setting

The St. George Library Center is the largest branch of the New York Public Library on Staten Island, one of the three boroughs of New York City served by the system. Besides offering a broad collection of circulating materials, print and audiovisual, for all ages, St. George is located in the Borough Center and serves as the site for a large collection of reference materials, periodicals, and electronic information services. The young adult collection provides resources for school assignments, recreational reading, and personal problem solving and development. Young adults using the collection are of varied ethnic, economic, and educational backgrounds: some from families that have lived on Staten Island for generations and others who have recently immigrated to the United States, sometimes from countries that have no public libraries.

Program Description

The Youth Board began in October 1991 as a way to provide an outlet for young-adult voices on Staten Island and to act as a conduit for teens to bring their concerns and observations to a broad audience. In doing so, the Youth Board literally lights up teen talent against the usually negative images of teenagers that are drawn by our media today. To reach these goals, the library purchased and installed an electronic sign board in the YA area and extended an open invitation to poets, songwriters, and rappers in the junior and senior high schools on Staten Island to submit their work. Youth Board submissions are displayed for no less than one week, and each contributor is thanked by letter for his or her work. Forty-four poems have been accepted as of this writing. To ensure continued participation, the Youth Board is promoted both within the St. George Library Center and in the other eleven branches on Staten Island as well as through outreach to schools and community organizations. Individual teens as well as teachers who bring the program into their classrooms as a creative writing assignment pick up Youth Board application forms.

As an ongoing program, the Youth Board has been relatively simple to initiate and maintain. The St. George YA librarian is responsible for programming the sign board, organizing a schedule for displaying the submissions, and sending out thank you letters to contributors. The diversity of the young adults of Staten Island is reflected in the cross-section of teens submitting work. The Youth Board program is important because it provides a public forum accessible to all teens. Its ongoing, open-invitation, and open-form design make the Youth Board appealing to young adults who are put off by the deadlines, submission criteria, and judging standard in many writing contests.

Funding

A one-line electronic sign board was purchased from a library supplies catalog with $350 of a larger grant from the Heckscher Foundation to the New York Public Library's Office of Work with Young Adults. Staff time and supplies are part of the regular library budget.

Contact Person

Andrew Parson, St. George Library Center, New York Public Library, 5 Central Avenue, Staten Island, NY 10301. (718) 442-8561

35.
Oliver Wolcott Library, Inc.

Litchfield, Connecticut

Idea

Four-week lecture-discussion-demonstration humanities program on the Civil War

Customers

Forty to fifty junior and senior high school students, two-thirds male, and some of their parents and teachers

Setting

Oliver Wolcott Library, Inc., is an independent library that serves as the public library for the historic town of Litchfield, a middle-class community of approximately 8,400 people (mostly Caucasian-American). The library has responded to the needs of the area by expanding services to include a wide variety of cultural, educational, and recreational programs and assuming the role of a community center. Offerings have included everything from preschool story series to poetry readings to a program on soap opera production by a local Emmy winner.

Program Description

Living the American Civil War: An Historical Experience for Young People was a four-week program series held in October and November 1993. The program's objectives were to

1. Attract young adults to the library in enthusiastic, independent pursuit of knowledge
2. Give those same students an insight into the conflict that determined the subsequent course of American history
3. Stimulate an interest in the study of history in general by giving it an immediacy and vitality that is not always apparent to students in a classroom setting

The four-week, after-school, one-hour program series featured Al Gambone, a popular Civil War authority, plus a presentation by the 27th Connecticut Regiment, a Civil War reenactment group. Topics included an introduction to the war, the Battle of Gettysburg, the reenactment, and Connecticut's role plus the lasting results of the conflict. Registration was required, but there was no registration fee. The audience arrived early to claim the best seats, and the number of young adults remained consistent throughout. The library received enthusiastic support from the schools, who helped distribute a program syllabus to each student in the targeted age group.

Young adults as well as their parents and teachers were all affected by this program. The young people experienced, many for the first time, the excitement and satisfaction of a self-motivated study. The parents, a few of whom joined the audience as the series progressed, expressed amazement at and delight in the fact that their children were capable of immersing themselves so deeply in any area of study. The teachers obviously saw many of their students in a new light and let Mr. Gambone and the YA librarian know that they planned to build on this momentum in corresponding social studies units.

The program series was judged a success because of the consistent attendance and because nearly all materials on related displays circulated. Even on the second Wednesday, when school was on half-day session and the students were dismissed at noon, they all came at 3:30. The best evaluation, however, came from the group of young people who approached the YA librarian as she was heading home after the last program and asked her when the library was planning to do something like that again.

Funding

A $750 Regional Advisors' Award from the Waterbury Foundation was spent as follows: $350 paid for the expert presenter; $200 bought twenty-four books, fiction and nonfiction, on the Civil War; and $200 purchased the nine-part PBS series on the Civil War produced by Ken Burns on video.

Contact Person

Nancie McCann, Children's and Young Adult Librarian, The Oliver Wolcott Library, Inc., 160 South Street, Box 187, Litchfield, CT 06759-0187. (203) 567-8030

36.
Rowan Public Library

Salisbury, North Carolina

Idea

Summer jobs workshop

Customers

Young adults, ages fourteen through eighteen

Setting

Rowan Public Library is a library system serving Rowan County, North Carolina, which has 110,605 residents, 83 percent Caucasian-American. The system comprises a headquarters facility in Salisbury; two branches; outreach services to the homebound; and Stories-to-Go, a bookmobile service that visits over thirty daycare centers a month. The collection consists of 154,794 volumes, 1,828 audio and 1,811 video recordings, and 661 subscriptions. A YA librarian position was established in 1985. There are 6,185 young adults ages fourteen through eighteen enrolled in the local public schools. YA services have included collection development, annotated bibliographies, after-school booktalks, library tours, a newsletter, and participation in the statewide Quiz Bowl program for high school students.

Program Description

A Summer Jobs Workshop for Young Adults was presented on Saturday, May 1, 1993, from 10:00 A.M. to noon at the headquarters facility of the library. The goals of the workshop were to impart specific information in three major areas:

1. Types of jobs available to teenagers of different ages
2. How to find and apply for jobs
3. The benefits of building a good work ethic

Workshop organizers recruited five speakers from local government and business who could talk about the realities of the working world. Their presentations were to meet the following objectives:

SUMMER JOBS WORKSHOP
for Young Adults
14-18 *(yes, you!)*

Speakers at this Workshop will cover such topics as:
- »what jobs are available for what ages (14-15, 16-17, 18-up)
- »desirable characteristics for employees
- »getting a work permit
- »labor laws as they affect young adults
- »taxes and deductions
- »applying for summer jobs through the Employment Securities Commission
- »want ads, resumés and interviews
- »building a good work ethic
- »benefits of doing well: job for next summer, references

It's on Saturday, May 1, 1993 from 10:00 am to 12:00 pm, in the Hurley Room at Rowan Public Library, 201 W. Fisher St., Salisbury, NC.

For more information please call the Young Adult Services Librarian at 638-3015.

Rowan Public Library

1. To identify the qualities employers seek in employees
2. To describe available jobs
3. To explain how to fill out such forms as W-4s and work permits
4. To explain how to answer want ads, prepare resumes, and excel in interviews and on the job

All of this preparation was intended to clarify teenagers' uncertainties about employment basics. The national debate during the spring of 1993 over Nannygate and other issues surrounding part-time employment provided a particularly timely incentive for such a program, especially since school guidance counselors contacted said that the schools did not offer general information programs on the topic. The counselors also supported the idea of the public library as an ideal centralized place for the program and volunteered to help publicize it at their schools. Publicity was also placed in newspapers, with local merchants, and with county agencies.

The five speakers included a representative from a major local employer, who asked "How many of you want to move out and live on your own?" She then proceeded to bring the audience down to earth with real-world facts about the cost of living and the correlations among education levels, job types, and salaries. A representative of the Department of Social Services then outlined the types of jobs available to teenagers by age ranges, and the labor laws affecting them. The county comptroller distributed W-4s, 1040-EZs, and North Carolina's D400-EZ form and demonstrated how to fill them out. A representative from the Employment Securities Commission used worksheets to show participants how to channel school, volunteer, and previous work experience into a resume format. A representative of a local temporary employment agency concluded the program with a presentation on reading and responding to want ads, crafting a resume, interviewing, and going to work. She emphasized the specifics of grooming, promptness, courtesy, and hard work, explaining how excelling at a summer job not only earns money but also garners good references for the future.

The program's success was measured by the level of attendance—sixty-five people, mostly teenagers, and a few parents. They asked numerous questions and filled out all the forms. About half turned in formal evaluation forms, and all were positive. The speakers said that, based on the program's high attendance, enthusiastic participation, and the ongoing need for such information, they thought the Summer Jobs Workshop for Young Adults should be an annual program and that they would be happy to return. It was put on the calendar for 1994.

Funding

The five volunteer speakers also provided all their own handouts: sample budgets, W-4s, tax forms, work permits, resume worksheets, and labor-law fact sheets. Staff time and publicity came from the regular library budget.

Contact Person

Kristine Mahood, Rowan Public Library, P.O. Box 4039, Salisbury, NC 28145-4039. (704) 638-3000

37.
Tucson-Pima Library

Tucson, Arizona

Idea

Orientation program for students entering middle or junior high school and their parents

Customers

Students in fifth and sixth grades

Setting

The program was offered at eleven branches of the Tucson-Pima Library (TPL) system, serving all of Pima County (9,188 square miles) with a main library, ten major and four small branches, two neighborhood center libraries, three mobile units, and the Pima County Jail Library. The population of Pima County is 75.2 percent Caucasian-American, 29.3 percent Hispanic-American, 4.3 percent African-American, 2.2 percent Asian-American, 2.6 percent Native American, and 16.7 percent other (percentages do not add up to 100 because of computation of Hispanic).

Young adult services and collections are planned by a YA Services Committee composed of a librarian from each of the eleven major libraries and one or two representatives from the smaller libraries. Since 1992 all TPL libraries have used community analyses to measure and analyze residents' needs for services. The YA services librarians supplement this information with input from school librarians and teachers as well as from young adults themselves. In 1991–92 there were over 18,000 fifth and sixth graders in the county—the target of the JHS program.

Program Description

Junior High Survival (JHS) has been sponsored annually at an average of eleven different libraries for over five years for students entering middle or junior high school and their parents. The program is coordinated by a subcommittee of the system's YA Services Committee, who work with the following social service agencies: Planned Parenthood, Help-on-Call, Our Town Family Center, La Frontera Center, and local law enforcement agencies. These agencies provide counselors, often volunteers, who present the different components of JHS. These workshop leaders address the fears and concerns of students about to make the transition from elementary to secondary schools to prepare them and their parents for the changes they are facing. Such preparation improves students' chances for success in school and at home and reduces the likelihood of involvement in destructive activities. Topics include friendships, self-esteem, decision making, time management, coping skills, peer pressure, and emotional and physical changes. The parent workshop describes the topics to be covered with the students and emphasizes the importance of good communication within the family. Techniques for coping with adolescent changes are also discussed.

Approximately four hundred students from different cultural, ethnic, and socioeconomic backgrounds participated in 1993. JHS is advertised to the target audience through elementary school classroom visits by TPL's YA librarians during the last month of school. It is publicized

Promotional brochure for middle school orientation program.

through flyers at every branch, a feature article in TPL's monthly calendar, and a press release to all local media. In 1993 it was featured in a newspaper article about summer youth programs and on a talk radio station. Parents receive a letter encouraging them to attend. Registration is limited to thirty students per program.

Each group of students attends two three-hour sessions held on consecutive days during the month before the beginning of the fall semester. There are discussions, group activities, and question-and-answer periods. There is an ice-breaking game at the beginning to introduce everyone and to help participants realize that it can be fun to meet new people. There are timed team exercises to develop team-building and time-management skills. The importance of following directions is subtly reinforced throughout the program. Leaders strengthen participants' self-esteem in all activities and discussions. The leaders emphasize that students are confronted by many choices and that it is important to make good decisions. Planned Parenthood conducts an open discussion about emotional and physical changes that occur during adolescence. Participants put their questions in writing for the leader to read, answer, and discuss. Law enforcement representatives in 1993 brought former gang members to talk about the downside of joining a gang and how to avoid gang involvement.

Each participant receives a folder in which to keep the handouts for the activities. The library provides bookmarks, a bibliography on teen issues, homework hints, a brochure of relevant community agencies, and a business card from the branch's young adult services librarian. At the end of each session, participants complete evaluation forms that provide feedback to fine tune the following year's program content and style. Evaluations have shown that JHS graduates feel that the program taught them something new and was worthwhile.

Funding

Regular library budget; social services agencies provide the workshop leaders

Contact Person

Laura Thomas Sullivan, Tucson-Pima Library Administration, P.O. Box 27470, Tucson, AZ 85726. (602) 791-4391

38.
West Baton Rouge Parish Library

Port Allen, Louisiana

Idea

General YA service program

Customers

Young adults, ages twelve through eighteen

Setting

West Baton Rouge, the smallest of Louisiana's parishes, lies along the Mississippi River directly west of the city of Baton Rouge. Over nineteen thousand people, including seventeen hundred young adults (about two-thirds Caucasian-American and one-third African-American with a few Asian-Americans), reside in this predominantly rural area. Agriculture, tourism, and the chemical industry provide the economic base. Twenty percent of the residents live below the poverty level. The library has an 11,250-square-foot facility in the parish seat and a medium-sized bookmobile, with a staff of four professionals and seven paraprofessionals. It is financed by a dedicated millage. Construction to add a young adult and juvenile wing that will expand the library by 4,500 square feet began in the spring of 1994.

Program Description

Pursuing Paper Pleasures is a multifaceted campaign to promote reading and market specially designed library programs, services, and collections to young adults. A YA librarian started in January 1993 and began a new program of service and activities designed to

1. Raise the visibility of the public library throughout the parish
2. Satisfy library service and collection needs
3. Support the local school effort to achieve educational excellence and to encourage communication between school and public library

In the summer, besides sports, West Baton Rouge has few organized activities for teenagers. The library sponsors summer workshops that provide teens with a unique opportunity to enrich their science and art experience and to increase their knowledge of personal care. During the school year, the library sponsors ACT, college financial aid, science, and social science fair workshops. In 1993, workshop catalogs were distributed to seventh, eighth, and ninth graders, and more than 200 teens participated in one or more of the library's fourteen free workshops for young adults. University professors, business people, and other professionals volunteered their time and expertise. All workshops were complemented by displays of library materials.

West Baton Rouge school library media centers are underfunded; approximately $8.50 to $9.00 in state and federal funds are allocated per

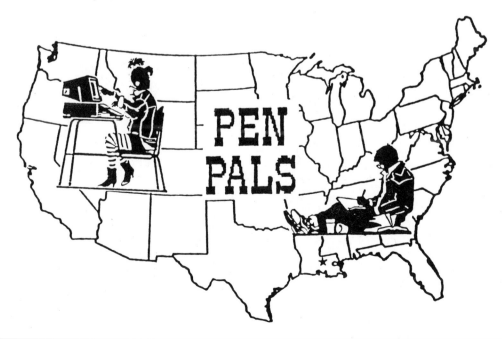

student for the purchase of library books and audiovisual materials. Since basic reference materials are lacking, so are library skills courses and even access for students to the media centers other than during study halls. To provide students with such library support and instruction, the public library offers teachers an assignment alert option and reserve shelves, student library skills courses and reference scavenger hunts. School library media specialists are offered interlibrary loan of materials for classroom use.

To promote reading, the library sponsors the Pursuing Paper Pleasures reading club and meet-the-author programs, and the YA librarian presents in-school booktalks and writes Good Reads annotations for marketing books in the library. A twenty-five-member Young Adult Advisory Board assists the YA librarian in planning, marketing, and evaluating the library's young adult services program. Advisory board members assist with workshop registration and housekeeping and also help create and arrange the Young Adult Zone, an area within the library to showcase hundreds of new hardback and paperback books and magazines for young adults.

In the fall, the YA librarian meets with each school faculty member to discuss cooperative possibilities to inspire teens to read, including the assignment alert forms and the reserve shelf option for research papers and class projects. In addition, a reading promotion program requested by the middle school library media specialists has become Reading for Contract. The YA librarian also provides classes with library skills instruction and booktalks in classrooms, arranges a meet-the-author program for gifted and talented students, and puts on a Library Scavenger Hunt to introduce students to basic reference sources. In response to the community D.A.R.E. program, the library serves as the resource center for drug abuse prevention information.

Funding

Regular library budget

Contact Person

Judy Boyce, Young Adult Librarian, West Baton Rouge Parish Library, 830 N. Alexander Avenue, Port Allen, LA 70767. (504) 342-7920, Ext. 27

39.
Wichita Public Schools, Unified School District 259

Wichita, Kansas

Idea

Authors program that is interactive, teleconferenced, multicultural

Customers

Middle and high school students as part of an overall K-twelve program

Setting

Unified School District 259, Wichita Public Schools, is composed of forty-eight thousand students (63 percent Caucasian-American, 21 percent African-American, 9 percent Hispanic-American, 5 percent Asian-American, 2 percent Native American) and is among the top seventy in size in the nation. Part of the district's mission statement emphasizes that the diversity of its student population is highly valued. Library Media Services (LMS), which is part of the district's Curriculum Services, has as its mission to ensure that students and teachers are effective users of information and ideas. Besides serving 103 K-twelve library media centers, LMS is also responsible for three cable television stations and one ITFS station.

Program Description

Multicultural Authors Week was organized as a districtwide grand sequel to a Multicultural Authors Call-In held earlier in the elementary schools. During one week an author a day was brought to Wichita. The objectives of the program were to

1. Acquaint students and teachers with a wide variety of authors of diverse ethnic backgrounds
2. Utilize books of authors and illustrators in ways that emphasize that their diversity strengthens their work in the same way that the diversity of the students is the strength of the district

3. Allow opportunity for all students to experience good literature at the level appropriate for them and to understand and appreciate the process of writing and illustrating
4. Network with other area institutions such as Wichita State University, the Wichita Public Library, and the parochial school system
5. Provide opportunity for minority students to experience and interact with positive role models in person and through their work

The week of programs involved a tightly scheduled combination of in-person school assembly appearances, live call-in programs in which authors interacted with students unable to get to assemblies, and collaborative programs for adult professionals and parents at cooperating institutions. Both Wichita Public Library and Wichita State University participated in hosting programs. Altogether, the program involved hundreds of adults and thousands of children, twelve hundred of them middle and high school students. Attendance at the author assemblies grew as the week progressed. The call-in programs had lines ringing all the time.

The program is currently being formally evaluated so it can be improved next year. Part of this year's success, however, was evident in having five authors who related so well to students, especially Gary Soto and Paula Underwood for young adults. Again and again minority students were drawn to the authors, proud to be so well represented and inspired to achieve greatness themselves. As a result of the success of the earlier telephone call-in programs that preceded Multicultural Authors Week, that program is being expanded to the middle schools in 1994.

Funding

The total funding of $8,000 included $4,500 from the Office of the Superintendent for Desegregation/Integration, $2,500 from the Crystal McNally Legacy, and the balance from the regular Library Media Services budget.

Contact Person

Rhita Muci, Library Media Specialist, Wichita Public Schools, Library Media Services Department, 3850 North Hydraulic, Wichita, KS 67219. (316) 833-2077

Reading Promotion

40.
Indianapolis–Marion County Public Library

Indianapolis, Indiana

Idea

Videotaped commercials for books for broadcast

Customers

Younger young adults, ages ten through fourteen

Setting

The Indianapolis–Marion County Public Library is a large, urban library system that includes a central library, twenty-one branches, and a bookmobile to serve 780,425 residents. For the ninth consecutive year, the library has experienced record-setting growth in collections, use, capital improvements, extended hours, and modernization. The library operates as its own tax district under an appointed board of community members. YA patrons are a high priority, served by both the adult and children's staff. Most locations have specially designated YA areas for materials with special spine labels, posters, book display units, and inviting seating.

Program Description

Teen Book Commercials was part of an effort to reach more young adolescents so as not to lose this group as readers and adult library users.

The Indianapolis–Marion County Public Library, in cooperation with the local PBS affiliate, WFYI-TV 20, offered a new component of the annual Summer Reading Program designed to appeal to and involve those ages ten to fourteen. The objective was to enhance the Summer Reading Program by selecting teens to contribute to the community as reading role models, sharing their reading interests and "selling" books to other teens via television, an important source for teen information.

A casting call was issued to all teen book lovers to sell their favorite book at library auditions for Teen Book Commercials. The project offered the teens an opportunity to have their opinions taken seriously in the community and to draw attention to themselves while being in a position of authority on a highly visible medium—television. The prestige of being a peer role model to promote reading and recommend books to other young adults was a powerful tool for involving teenagers in local literacy efforts. The message sent by teens for teens was considered far more likely to have legitimate impact than any other form of reading endorsement.

Auditions were scheduled at the central library and all branch locations for neighborhood access to the program. To help students prepare for the audition, a tip sheet was distributed and a sample video was made available for preview at each library. During July 1993 two Children's Services Office staff members traveled throughout the system taping the auditions. Each teen who auditioned earned fifty points in IMCPL's incentive-based Summer Reading Program. These points, and all points earned by reading books, could be exchanged for unique prizes specifically chosen for teens. WFYI staff reviewed the auditions and selected thirty that demonstrated potential. The emphasis was not on polished, professional acting but on students' enthusiasm combined with the ability to convey what they liked about their books. Winners were notified in August, and the taping sessions for the on-air commercials took place at WFYI before the start of school. The commercials air during the after-school hours, 3:30 to 6:00 P.M., between PBS programs.

In total, 143 teens (87 female, 56 male) presented their forty-five-second commercial auditions. In conjunction with the 1993 Summer Reading Report, a written evaluation will be produced that will include a statistical analysis and recommendations for improving the project next summer. Preliminary analysis, especially participation by age group, indicates that the Teen Book Commercials program was a factor in summer reading participation for this age group, which increased from 29 percent in 1992 to 31 percent in 1993. The project proved to be a cost effective and effective way to involve teens in summer recreational reading.

Funding

Regular library budget. Studio and air time donated by WFYI-TV20

Contact Person

Christine Cairo, Coordinator of Children's Services, Indianapolis–Marion County Public Library, Library Service Center, 2450 North Meridian Street, Indianapolis, IN 46208. (317) 269-1775

41.
Miami-Dade Public Library System

Miami, Florida

Idea

Outreach school visits, booktalks

Customers

Ninth-grade students in all Dade County public and private schools

Setting

The Miami-Dade Public Library System serves a population of 1.6 million people with thirty-one branches and a main library. An international and multicultural community, Dade County celebrates diversity with a population that is 49 percent Hispanic-American, 25 percent Caucasian-American, 22 percent African-American, and includes an increasing number of Asian-Americans. Recent immigrants from Haiti, Central and South America, and a winter-intensive Canadian population have intensified the multilingual atmosphere in a community where Spanish, French, and Creole vie with English in everyday conversation.

Program Description

Connect Nine is an outreach program offered by the Miami-Dade Public Library Young Adult Management Team to all Dade County ninth graders in public and private schools. The purpose of the program is to encourage these young adults to read for pleasure, familiarize them with available library services for homework and personal use, and connect them face to face with librarians. The program's objectives are to

1. Present booktalks about high quality YA fiction and nonfiction with appeal and interest for ninth-grade students
2. Introduce students to materials available in

all branches, such as career information; job search, college, university, and vocational materials; and audiovisual materials such as videos, CDs, and audiocassettes

Ninth graders were selected as the target audience for Connect Nine because this is their first year in high school. Recognizing that this is an ideal time when students are receptive to new experiences, the YA librarians reach out to them with booktalks, share such necessary library information as how to get library cards, and attempt to bridge the gap in the passage between childhood and adulthood.

Letters are sent in the fall to all schools with ninth grades, inviting the English teachers or school library media specialists to reserve a time for a school visit. The letter includes information about what services are available for the visit. Appointments are made in the months of October, November, December, February, March, and April, during which the YA staff has set aside certain days for outreach so that the branch managers can schedule properly. A normal school visit takes about forty-five minutes, or a regular school period. During this time students are introduced to fifteen to twenty fiction and nonfiction books through booktalks. A team of two YA staff visits together to make the program and style of presentation more varied. Different kinds of materials are selected for each visit. Sometimes teachers request poetry or a theme, such as black history. Whenever possible, the requests are honored, and other AV materials are brought along for display. One of the librarians likes to bring popular music and let the students guess the name of the artist and songs. Another uses storytelling to entice them with horror and gross exaggerations, to which teens respond well. Each person develops a unique style. Bibliographies listing the books presented as well as other good choices are provided to the school's library media specialist.

Since Connect Nine's inception in 1992–93, approximately 5,560 ninth graders in twenty-one schools have been visited. The success of the program is measured in the way students visit branches after the class visits and request the titles that have been presented, although a strict count is not kept. Perhaps success can best be seen in the actual words of one Hispanic-American student who expressed his thanks to the YA librarians by saying, "This presentation has opened new vistas for me."

Funding

Funding is part of the library budget; the outreach visit is conducted during the regular work day. There are no additional costs except for mileage if staff use their own cars. In many cases, the library provides a staff car. Each branch has a YA budget. The YA paperback budget covers replacement and purchase of multiple copies of titles presented in booktalks.

Contact Person

Helen Vandersluis, Young Adult Services Manager, Miami-Dade Public Library System, 101 W. Flagler Street, Miami, FL 33173. (305) 375-5577

MIAMI-DADE PUBLIC LIBRARY SYSTEM

An Outreach Program presented by the Young Adult Department of the Miami-Dade Public Library System

ATTENTION ALL NINTH GRADE ENGLISH TEACHERS

The Miami-Dade Public Library would like to come to your school and present book talks letting students know more about their neighborhood library and what it has to offer them.

This program is targeted for 9th Grade English classes with students in transition from middle school to senior high school.

The purpose of the program is to:
  *Encourage students to read for pleasure;
  *Make connection with students;
  *Make students aware of library resources which are available to them for homework and as well as for personal informational needs.

October, November, February, March, April, 1994

For more information, or to schedule a Library-School Connection presentation for your classes, contact the Young Adult Librarian at your nearest library location, listed below:

CORAL GABLES BRANCH LIBRARY

3443 Segovia Street
442-8706 Alice Connors-Suarez

MAIN LIBRARY

101 West Flagler Street
375-2665 Helen Vandersluis or Gina Moon

MIAMI BEACH BRANCH LIBRARY

2100 Collins Avenue
535-4219 Teresa Morrell

NORTH DADE REGIONAL LIBRARY

2455 NW 183 Street
625-6424 Jacqui Sturdivant

NORTHEAST BRANCH LIBRARY

2030 Aventura Blvd.
931-5512 Joe Weeks

SOUTH DADE REGIONAL LIBRARY

10750 SW 211 Street
375-5577 Leonie Waltherr

WEST DADE REGIONAL LIBRARY

9445 Coral Way
553-1134 Mike Power

WEST KENDALL REGIONAL LIBRARY

10201 Hammocks Boulevard
375-5231 Susannah Oberheiser

SW131/93

METRO-DADE

Printed on Recycled Paper

42.
River Valley Middle School Media Center, Greater Clark County Schools

Jeffersonville, Indiana

Idea

Reading promotion, multiple activities

Customers

Middle school students, grades six through eight

Setting

River Valley Middle School students come from a range of economic, social, and cultural backgrounds in southern Indiana close to the banks of the Ohio River. The student body of 840 in 1993 was 69 percent Caucasian-American, 30 percent African-American, and 1 percent Asian- and Hispanic-American. Approximately 30 percent qualify for free or reduced-price lunch. School programs to meet varied student abilities include ongoing at-risk, academically advanced, collaborative special education, and annual fine arts, environmental, and career programs. A wide variety of electives, including new reading-related electives, is offered to seventh and eighth graders.

Program Description

Reading: The First Piece of the Puzzle was designed as a student-reading-motivation program to meet three targeted needs:

1. A time and place to read
2. Materials to read
3. Actually seeing reading role models

A wide range of activities was developed to provide opportunities to meet these needs throughout the entire school. Participation could be as an individual, a member of a small group, a class member, or a member of one of the twelve academic teams. All activities were made optional, although a number of teachers incorporated specific reading challenges into

An eighth-grade student in the Book Buddies class reads to Wilson Elementary students.

their curriculum. Everyone in the school, including the seventy-five adult staff members, participated in at least one event.

Reading: The First Piece of the Puzzle was an important element of school life in 1993, with multiple impacts at different levels. From the students who raced to check out copies of *Short & Shivery* for their team's read aloud, to the students who brought in souvenirs from Kenya for the African-American Day Read-In, each event found students enthusiastically involved in reading. The project also tied together all of the special events and days celebrated at school. The annual fine arts and environmental programs, of which the school is very proud, were united by a puzzle theme. Both the art and industrial technology classes created puzzles based on books. Math classes incorporated word puzzles into their lessons. New elective classes on reading, called "Reading Is Fun," "Puzzles and Games," and "Book Buddies," were created and will remain a permanent part of the curriculum. Bookmarks promoting books and events, along with a commemorative banner, were created by the media aides class.

The Jeffersonville Township Public Library YA librarian worked with the middle school in freeing up storytelling time for the Book Buddies and math lab classes to read to younger children on four different occasions. The twenty math lab students created counting books for preschoolers and then visited the public library to read their creations during story times. The public library also sponsored an author appearance by Doreen Rappaport. Teachers at Wilson Elementary School arranged pairings between their students and River Valley students for the Book Buddies class, and this was one of the most successful elements of the project. The class visited the elementary school eleven times to read and talk about books and read to the younger children. Seventh and eighth graders also read to sixth grade students at various times within the middle school itself, serving as older reading role models. Other activities included weekly sustained silent reading by all students and staff, student input on books considered for purchase in the school library media center, themed read-ins, guest adult readers, a rain forest reading challenge that raised over $150 to help save the rain forest, and a summer reading program.

Reading: The First Piece of the Puzzle was listed in *The Best of the Network 1993*, published by Middle Grades Reading Network, University of Evansville, 1800 Lincoln Avenue, Evansville, IN 47722. As reading and science teacher Linda Bentley put it, "I think this project was extremely effective, and my students and I were delighted to be a part of it."

Funding

The project received a $5,000 Reading Network grant from the Lilly Endowment for reading materials, supplies, and incentives, plus $1,000 from the Parent Teacher Organization for T-shirts, pencils, and book gift certificates. Three parents helped with activities; fifty adults spoke on the importance of reading at Career Day, and twelve adults volunteered their time as guest readers. The Jeffersonville Township Public Library supported an author visit, and environmental materials were donated by the Indiana Soil and Conservation Department. The school has received a subsequent $14,000 grant to promote individual reading, also from the Lilly Endowment.

Contact Person

Eden Kuhlenschmidt, Media Specialist, River Valley Middle School, 2220 New Albany-Charleston Road, Jeffersonville, IN 47130. (812) 288-4848

43.
Salado Middle School Library, East Central Independent School District

San Antonio, Texas

Idea

Readers' club

Customers

Middle school students, grades six through eight

Setting

Salado Middle School is on the southeast side of San Antonio with approximately sixty staff members and 850 students who are almost equally divided among Caucasian-American, African-American, and Hispanic-American ethnicity. Most come from families of middle or lower income levels. The school has recently begun team teaching at all grade levels with students rotating exclusively among five core teachers and various elective teachers.

Program Description

The Salado Technology and Reading Society (STARS) began as a reading incentive program in the spring of 1991 and grew into a reading club. STARS goals include developing reading incentive programs, recognizing student achievement, and guiding the relationship between libraries and literacy with the objectives of improving test scores and creating lifelong readers. All students are eligible to join, although by policy Salado students may join only one club. Members must maintain passing grades and satisfactory conduct to participate in any Salado club activities. STARS students read to young children in an after-school program called Prime Time, read to homeless children and donate new books to their school at the San Antonio Metropolitan Mission, have read-ins, reading rallies, TV turn-offs, holiday video programs, field trips, campus beautification projects, adopt-a-shelf programs, and guest speakers. STARS members also sponsor a reading incentive program called All Star Readers. Students read and review books from the Salado Library Media Center, and their reviews are published in the school paper. Students also participate in recognition celebrations and win prizes. All Star celebrations have included such guests as the Spurs' David Robinson and Mayor Nelson Wolff.

STARS members have visited the Witte Museum, IMAX Theater, St. Mary's University Library, Ripley's Believe It or Not, the San Antonio Riverwalk, and Fiesta Texas. The club also offers Curiosity Classes to the entire student body. Students select the topics, and community members teach the classes. Popular classes have covered karate and reptiles. Goliath, a twelve-foot python, has been the most popular guest.

Another special event was a visit with author Joan Lowery Nixon, in which students, the school superintendent, club sponsors, and parents rode a river barge and enjoyed a Mexican dinner with her. She gave each student an autographed book and spoke about her writing. Nixon was so impressed with the program that she subsequently mentioned it during an appearance at the International Reading Association Conference in May 1993.

The STARS club is sponsored by the school library media specialist, two reading teachers, a journalism teacher, the coach and typing teacher, and a computer aide. Parents serve as drivers, chaperones, and the refreshment committee. Evaluation takes place continuously. Student involvement, library circulation, improved test scores, and an overflowing library are measures of STARS' success.

Funding

A $450 grant from the H.E.B. grocery store chain funded the Joan Lowery Nixon dinner. Other funds have included mini-grants from the East Central Foundation, $500 from Gov. Anne Richards's grant to Salado Middle School, and various fundraisers such as book fairs, carnation sales, and school dances. Parents volunteer time.

Contact Person

Bonnie Rice, Salado Middle School, 3602 South W.W. White, San Antonio, TX 78222. (210) 648-3310

44.
Wymore Career Education Center, Orange County Schools

Eatonville, Florida

Idea

Introducing children's literature and reading to teenage parents

Customers

At-risk teenage parents, grades seven through twelve

Setting

Wymore is the alternative middle and high school for the district, serving an 85 percent minority population, all of whom have been designated at risk and none of whom has succeeded in a traditional school setting. Students come from dysfunctional households and are at least one grade behind; many have dropped out of school at least once, had run-ins with law enforcement, or both. Eighty-seven percent receive free or reduced-cost lunches. Since the school is the only one of its type in the county, students are bused as far as thirty miles, some riding more than an hour each way. Wymore has small classes, vocational courses, and many special programs, including Compact, which provides mentors; LEAP, which offers scholarships; dual enrollment, which gives students access to technical schools; and work study programs. The teen-parent program has a nursery to help keep teen mothers in school.

Program Description

Breaking the Cycle is an ongoing program developed by the media specialist and the teen-parent teacher. With a goal of helping teen parents prepare their children for school, the program introduces the world of children's literature to teen parents and discusses the importance of reading to their children. Most of the sixty or more Wymore teen parents are poor readers

Book covers were made using computers.

themselves and come from homes with no books and no role models for reading. The program has two objectives. The teen parents will

1. Become familiar with a body of quality children's literature
2. Share books with their children

The teen-parent teacher and the media specialist hope to break the nonreading cycle and give both students and their children a helping hand for the future.

Each week the media specialist visits the teen-parent classroom, bringing examples of quality children's books, many of which have multicultural themes. She and the students read the books together and discuss how to use them with their children. The session begins with fingerplays and nursery rhymes, then moves to simple picture books, concept books, fairy tales, and so on. The students and presenter discuss and compare illustrations. The books are then left with the students for at least a week. There is a children's literature collection in the media center, and students are also taken to the public library to obtain cards and check out books. One of the highlights of the program is the creation by the students of at least one book for their children. In most cases, these are the first books ever owned by parent or child. One student told of her toddler actually sleeping with his book. Students also help make puppets to use for storytelling with their children.

Evaluation takes many forms. Circulation of the media center's children's collection has been increasing steadily, and students show increased familiarity with many favorite titles in children's literature. The public librarian was amazed at their knowledge of children's books and stories when they visited the public library. Discussions with students about how they are reading and sharing books with their youngsters is ongoing. Every student has completed at least one book, staying on task for over a month, which is rare for at-risk students, and they are proud of their accomplishments. An unforeseen bonus of the program has been the improvement of the students' own reading skills. Reading to their babies has given them an excellent opportunity to practice reading themselves. The media specialist considers this one of the most rewarding experiences of a thirty-two-year career.

Funding

The program is funded from the regular school and library media center budget. The majority of the books are borrowed from the public library.

Contact Person

Elaine Ann Apter, Media Specialist, Wymore Career Education Center, 100 East Kennedy Boulevard, Eatonville, FL 32751. (407) 644-7518, ext. 208

Special Needs Populations

45.
Broward County Libraries

Pembroke Pines, Florida

Idea

Ongoing program series for young adults with special needs

Customers

Young adults, ages ten through eighteen

Setting

The South Regional–Broward Community College Library, one of four regional libraries within the twenty-eight libraries of the Broward County Library System, serves an urban population of more than 1 million people, of whom 11 percent fall within the ages of ten through eighteen. The South Regional Library is the only one of the four that is paired with a community college library, and in addition, it is a depository for materials and services for the deaf and visually impaired. Many users come only for those services.

Program Description

Ready, Willing, and Able, and Possibilities were two summer programs in an ongoing series for disabled young adults—remembering that physical and emotional age are not always synonymous. The program goals were to

1. Encourage disabled young adults and their parents to view the library as their place (as well as a place for able-bodied people) by having events specifically for them to which the general public was also invited
2. Promote a better understanding of disabilities overall

National statistics show that one out of every seven persons in the United States is disabled. This ongoing series for disabled young adults is aimed to make them feel welcome to participate in this or in any other library event or activity. The July program, Ready, Willing, and Able, presented an afternoon of motivational speakers from all areas of life who had either overcome their disability or had risen above it. Possibilities, held in August, was a program of inspirational music about overcoming obstacles, with both able-bodied and physically challenged participants.

One hundred and twenty inquiries resulted in the George Jenkins Foundation grant. Next, staffers identified speakers and performers who were either disabled or had overcome their disability and contacted them through cold calling. They were asked to convey how they faced their disability and to encourage others to do the same. Some people cried and some were belligerent because they had not yet reached that stage; they were thanked for their time but not used in the program. The eight eventually selected came from all walks of life—singers, a comedian, a lawyer, a former television newsman, and an actor-director (who later would direct and coproduce Possibilities). Publicity was faxed or mailed to all surrounding agencies dealing with disabilities, with phenomenal response.

Approximately seventy-five people came—in busloads, private wheelchair taxis, with Seeing Eye dogs—nothing stopped them! All disabilities were well represented. One teenager who had come with his father hugged the librarian afterward and cried because he had attempted suicide the night before but felt so inspired by everyone's stories that he wanted to try to put his life back on track again. (His father cried, too.) The video of this program is being edited for circulation to the public.

The first program cost no extra library money because of the generosity of the presenters in donating their time. All the grant money paid for props, a choreographer, and a cast party for "Possibilities: A Musical Montage by Exceptional Teens," which played to a full house of over 400 people with standing ovations. In all, thirty-six teens and family members participated in what the librarian fondly called "acting lessons." It was difficult to find parents willing to set aside their natural protectiveness of their disabled children, but eventually three were allowed to participate, one with muscular dystrophy, one mildly retarded, and a third with Down syndrome. At first everyone was terrified of each other, but by the end of four weeks of rehearsals, participants were helpful, sharing, and loving toward one another and tearful at the end, wanting to know when the next production was scheduled! A third program was being planned for the holidays as this was submitted, with the local agencies far more receptive to the library's efforts because they realized that their clients were not going to be hurt or exploited but just be a part of the larger society as regular library patrons like everybody else.

Funding

The program was supported by $1,000 from the George Jenkins Foundation (Jenkins was the founder of the Publix food stores). All speakers and performers donated their time. Staff time and publicity came out of the regular library budget.

Contact Person

Laurie Shaina Latimer, Young Adult Librarian, South Regional–Broward Community College Library, Division of Youth Services, 7300 Pines Boulevard, Pembroke Pines, FL 33024. (305) 963-8821

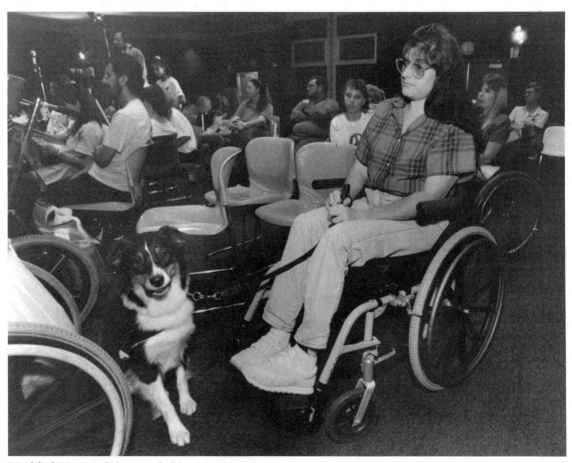

Disabled young adult attends library program. (Photo used with permission of *The Miami Herald.*)

Youth Participation

46.
Berkeley Public Library

Berkeley, California

Idea

Employing young adults in the library

Customers

Three high school students

Setting

The Berkeley Public Library serves the city of Berkeley with a central library, four neighborhood branches, and a Tool Lending Library. Its 210 employees fill 120.13 full-time equivalent positions to serve ninety-two thousand registered borrowers. The library is open sixty-four hours a week and experiences more than 1.4 million visits annually. The library serves a population of 104,200 (60 percent Caucasian-American, 20 percent African-American, 14 percent Asian-American, 9 percent Hispanic-American). Just under 10 percent of the population is of school age (five through seventeen). There is a wide range of income levels in this university town, and about 16 percent of the community lives below the poverty line. In 1989 the library institutionalized young adult services by hiring five young adult librarians—one for each branch and one for Central. YA services include special collections at each location, systemwide programming, and site-specific projects. The materials budget for young adult books and music is $14,000. Programs are funded by gift money from the Friends of the Library.

Program Description

In response to a well-executed needs assessment that relied heavily on teen input, Berkeley Public Library employed three high school students who worked at three different locations throughout the system from 1991 until 1993. The goals of the program were to

1. Provide employment and job training for three high school students
2. Honor the library's mandate of public service to young adults

By designing programs, contributing to outreach projects, and advising librarians, the student workers helped make services more responsive to teenagers.

Primarily a training position designed for high school students, the job at BPL involved four components: public service orientation, clerical work, computer literacy, and outreach. Students worked closely with YA librarians and assumed responsibility for the physical upkeep of areas at each BPL location exclusively dedicated to high school students. The public service component ranks first on the list because the library stresses the importance of courtesy and fair treatment of all patrons. Through the clerical component the student worker learned the basics of office work—filing, inventory, operating office machines, preparing mailings, and processing books as well as audiovisual materials. Including a computer literacy component ensured that the student learned the rudiments of database manipulation, data entry, and word processing. The outreach component made the job classification special. Among other activities, student workers produced the Rap and Poetry Jam (an evening of music and poetry), and they also represented BPL at many community events including Cinco de Mayo and Juneteenth. They addressed the entire staff as panelists at a systemwide in-service training program that focused on staff interactions with teenagers in the library (see no. 3 in this publication), and they reviewed collections and participated in BPL's Young Adult Advisory Committee.

For the student workers themselves the project offered opportunities to develop a variety of job skills, including the experience of working in a multicultural environment and an introduction to public service and computer proficiency. Two of the students still attend high school and work elsewhere; one now attends a local community college. For the library itself the project spurred the institution to better serve its teenage clientele. This became evident in collection development and also in heightened sensitivity among the staff. As an institution the library also benefitted from active coalitions and partnerships with other youth-serving agencies. Finally, in a small but significant way, hiring the student workers enlarged the pool of library staff to include traditionally underrepresented people and nudged the library forward on its mission to diversify its own staff.

The measure of student performance took place on three levels. On a practical level, the students did their jobs well; they and the young-adult librarians with whom they worked felt satisfied with job performance. From the point of view of library management, including branch supervisors, the students made very practical contributions to the individual sites. The Board of Library Trustees' positive evaluation of the project led to the creation of three student-worker jobs beginning fiscal year 1993–94.

Currently, three new student workers carry on and expand the work of their grant-funded predecessors. This movement in the direction of inclusion promises better service to young adults in Berkeley. Students find more of what they want and need at the library, and the institution profits from the infusion of youthful energy and ideas.

Funding

In 1991, an LSCA grant project designed to improve library services to young adults at risk

Young adult library employee Kim McCombs displays some of her work.

provided funds to conduct the initial needs assessment and seed money for service plans. Since unemployment, especially the disproportionate rate for African-American and Latino teenagers, ranked high on everyone's list of concerns, the library created specialized jobs for teens through a partnership with another city of Berkeley agency, the Real Alternatives Project (RAP). The library provided job sites, training, and 50 percent of salary costs. RAP screened applicants and matched BPL's financial contribution. The total salary cost to the library equaled $5,000.

Contact Person

Kay Finney, Berkeley Public Library, South Branch, 1901 Russell Street, Berkeley, CA 94703. (510) 644-6860

47.
Broward County Libraries

Plantation, Florida

Idea

Young adult library advisory board; YA-planned programs

Customers

Young adults, ages twelve through eighteen

Setting

The Broward County West Regional Library is a large facility located just west of Fort Lauderdale in the fast-growing city of Plantation, population sixty-eight thousand. One of three regional libraries in the Broward County system, West Regional has an extensive collection of print and audiovisual materials for all ages, plus a large reference collection.

Program Description

From Our Library to You is an ongoing collection of teen programs and services aimed at Plantation residents of all ages as well as the library staff, completely planned and executed by young adults through a group called the West Regional Young Adult Library Advisory Board (LAB). The group was formed by the assistant head of youth services at the library. The goals of LAB are to

1. Provide an opportunity for individual leadership and job experience for teens
2. Encourage involvement in the library for social, recreational, and research purposes
3. Offer ways for teens to communicate with their community
4. Establish an awareness of the nature and needs of that community

LAB makes the library a viable place for young adults in terms of their needs and thus encourages library use.

LAB programs and services are decided at brainstorming sessions held at the library in March and August. All LAB members attend these meetings, as does their library sponsor. Once ideas are adopted, action committees are formed, and teens carry out the plans. Any official letters, publicity, or public service announcements are created by the staff sponsor. Follow-up meetings are held every six weeks to discuss results, additional plans, and problems. Meanwhile, the communications chairperson contacts members of the LAB executive committee as well as the membership in order to monitor progress. Each program or service is evaluated by LAB and the staff sponsor as soon as it is completed. In 1993 LAB voted to limit itself to thirty members, but not every member participates in every activity. There is something for everyone to do.

LAB-planned and executed activities, with their audience counts, have been as follows:

Recreational

- Annual dance parties in 1992 and 1993, with music from a local high school the first year and a DJ from a radio station the second. Attendance: 110, 130 teens
- Teen Jeopardy. Attendance: 97 teens
- Junior Jeopardy, created by request for children ages nine through twelve. Attendance: 127 children and parents
- A design and paint your own T-shirt program. Attendance: 41 teens
- A computer games night. Attendance: 52 teens
- Moonwalk, a night of games for children ages five through ten. Attendance: 139 children and adults

Informational

- Annual college night, with representatives of five Florida colleges

Service

- Library aides to perform clerical and craft duties in the Youth Services Department
- Donations for Covenant House
- Peer tutoring of other teens in all school subjects, grade levels six through twelve
- Technology aides, trained by library staff to help patrons in the use of library technology

Community

- An Earth Day celebration, for which LAB created and decorated an official proclamation, persuaded the public to sign it, and then presented it to the Plantation City

Council, where it was read aloud by the mayor. The teens also planted in front of the library a tree donated by a local nursery.

Other related actvities

- *Listen Up!* an annual magazine written, edited, and published by LAB
- A booktalking video written, directed, produced, and filmed by LAB for use in area middle schools
- A Best Teen Picks recommended reading list created by LAB and maintained in the YA section of the library

The LAB program is evaluated by public response, such as letters from LAB parents and from people whose lives LAB members have touched. The LAB teens, also highly multicultural, well represent the many ethnic groups in the community and thus contribute to interethnic friendships. Audience statistics and the constant demand for LAB membership also suggest that LAB is a valuable, rewarding, and self-perpetuating activity that, in an era of youth gangs, is a means of using a dynamite human resource—teens in the library!

The LAB sponsor has been promoted to head of youth services at a new branch, and the West Regional YA LAB teens are going there to help her open the new library and recruit a new LAB group for that community.

Funding

The LAB program is supported by regular library budget for staff time plus partial funding from the Friends of the Library. In addition, LAB fund-raising efforts have included a teen book sale and an international food fair and bake sale enthusiastically supported by the public, bringing $290 into the LAB program fund. All items were donated by the community or made by LAB members.

Contact Person

Leila J. Sprince, Youth Services Department, North Regional Broward Community College Library, 1100 Coconut Creek Boulevard, Coconut Creek, FL 33066. (305) 968-2469 or 2420

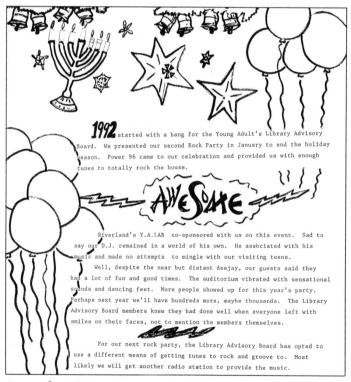

A page from *Listen Up.*

48.
Emporia Public Library

Emporia, Kansas

Idea

Discussion series to help young African-American men approach adulthood

Customers

African-American young men, ages fourteen through eighteen

Setting

Emporia is a city of twenty-seven thousand (2 percent African-American) in the east central part of Kansas. The Emporia Public Library, established in 1869, serves residents of Emporia and the seven surrounding counties with ten full-time and nine part-time employees. The library has a collection of one hundred and seven thousand volumes, experiences an annual circulation of approximately three hundred thousand, and was used by two hundred and ten thousand people in 1993. Joint programs between the library and Emporia State University are common, especially with the university's ALA-accredited library school. The university, one of six Regents' universities in Kansas, has an enrollment of sixty-one hundred students.

Program Description

Rites of Passage was a straightforward program in which twenty-five young African-American men met twice a week during June and July 1993 to talk. The idea for the program came from a young African-American man in Emporia who asked his father, an administrator at Emporia State University, whether he was an "endangered species." The father, shaken by his son's question, asked the library director if a joint library-university program could be developed to help his son and other minority young men and women. The goals of the program were to

1. Help participants plan a positive future
2. Help participants cope with daily problems ranging from racism to parenthood
3. Provide opportunities to meet successful African-American adult men from professions other than athletics who could serve as role models

No brochures were distributed, and advertising was done only through bulletin boards, on

Award certificate

cable television, and in churches. Enrollment forms were available in the library. There were no bibliographies distributed, only honest talk. There were no "canned" speeches. Moderators demanded hard-edged discussion, and all efforts focused on helping young people evaluate and plan their lives. Topics discussed were self-esteem, peer pressure, racism, role models, self-determination, sexual relationships and responsibilities, parenthood responsibilities, male and female roles, employment opportunities, racism in employment, social outlets and conditions, goal setting, and post-secondary educational opportunities.

The program was cosponsored with Emporia State University with meetings held at the public library. Thirteen speakers were recruited on a volunteer basis by the university's director of the Office of Minority Affairs, and programs were coordinated with the library director. Each meeting addressed a specific topic and was moderated by African-American men (for example, businessmen, clergymen, academic administrators, and educators). These men were recruited because it was felt that the young men needed to see African-American role models other than athletes.

There was no formal evaluation other than the result that, in a city where African-Americans make up only 2 percent of the population, twenty-five young African-American men spent three hours on summer afternoons in a public library discussing their futures. The library will now be offering programs for young African-American women and young Mexican-American men and women in 1994 because of the program's success. All programs will be offered on an annual basis thereafter. Nationwide stories carried by both the Associated Press and the library press, as well as stories in local media, have produced requests for information about the program from cities across the country. Sen. Robert Dole sent a letter of congratulations, writing, "There are few more important tasks than ensuring that our youth have role models who will help them in achieving rewarding and productive lives."

Funding

The regular library budget supported the program. Speakers donated their time and were paid only travel expenses.

Contact Person

Howard F. McGinn, Director, Emporia Public Library, 110 East Sixth Avenue, Emporia, KS 66801. (316) 342-6524

49.
Middletown Township Public Schools

Middletown, New Jersey

Idea

Library sleep-in

Customers

Tenth-grade honors history class

Setting

The Middletown High School Library North serves a student population of over 1,750 plus a teaching staff of approximately two hundred in a comprehensive high school. Media Center staff include one educational media specialist, a media technician, a secretary, and one or two outstanding parent and student volunteers. During 1992–93, 694 classes visited the library, more than ten thousand students on passes signed in, and more than ten thousand books circulated. At the time of the sleep-in, an online catalog and CD-ROM network were being installed. A strong serial collection includes *INFOTRAC, Newsbank, SIRS*, the *New York Times Index, DIALOG's Knowledge Index,* and interlibrary loan access through Palinet and New Jersey's Region V Library Cooperative.

Program Description

Election Night Sleep-In, November 3, 1992, was the culminating activity of two months of research by the tenth grade honors history class. The goal was to involve students in the election so that they would develop the skills they will need to become informed voters in the years ahead. The sleep-in was a unique way to generate enthusiasm, not only for the 1992 presidential election, but also for the important role of the individual in American politics. The social studies teacher had used this program several years before in a junior high school with ninth grade civics students and wondered with the media specialist whether it would appeal to tenth graders in a high school setting. Another teacher who had been part of the junior high team helped to chaperone the event.

Students were introduced to the project by their social studies teacher. They were required to predict the percentage of popular votes the candidates would receive in each state. The research process involved comparing the voting histories of the states and evaluating the impact of campaign issues and platforms on each state's voters. After analyzing their research, students were required to predict the 1992 outcome and provide justification for their predictions. As part of their research, the students used books, almanacs, a daily vertical file of news clippings, the latest periodicals, *INFOTRAC, Newsbank,* and a variety of other reference sources. Homework was to keep up with nightly newscasts and polls, which provided information for daily class discussions. Relevant materials were kept separate on a book truck to organize materials for easier student access. Students evaluated resources in terms of the importance of each as well as the quality and usefulness of the information retrieved. On election night students presented their findings on an overhead projector to the class, keeping up with results as they became available via news coverage from the three major networks.

Refreshments consisted of soda, homemade cookies, and pizza. The two teachers and the media specialist separated boys and girls on different sides of the room, stationed themselves in the middle, and turned off the lights around 1:30 A.M. Most students slept on the floor in sleeping bags, but one or two chose tables. (As befitting her age and station, the library media specialist commandeered the only couch.) An hour later the giggles subsided. Student comments included, "I don't believe I'm sleeping in the library," and "I don't believe I'm sleeping with boys/girls and my mother gave her permission!" Early the next morning, after a quick breakfast of doughnuts, juice, and hot chocolate provided by the library, some students went home to shower and change while others headed for the locker rooms. Sleeping bags and other gear were stored in the conference room, the building "safe" for valuables. The students who went out of their way to participate in the sleep-in will vote in the 1996 presidential election. The hope of this program was that the enthusiasm they experienced and the understanding they gained in 1992 will carry over in the patterns they will establish as educated voters.

Funding

Support for this event was a cooperative effort among teachers, parents, and students. The social studies teacher provided T-shirts reading "Election '92 Sleep-In MTHS North," with pictures of a donkey and an elephant, to unify the group and lend focus to the event. The president of the Parent Faculty Association contributed campaign decorations through the Middletown League of Women Voters. Teachers and administrators helped chaperone. Parents dropped in, as did building custodians to debate politics. TV production students helped set up the videos, which required over 100 feet of cable hookup, and then filmed the students talking about the election. A student from the journalism class slept over to provide press coverage for *The Lion's Roar,* the school paper.

Contact Person

Jayne Frye, Educational Media Specialist, Middletown High School North Library, 63 Tindall Road, Middletown, NJ 07701. (908) 706-6078

Election night sleepover flyer.

50.
New York Public Library

New York, New York

Idea

Summer group activity creating a mural for the library

Customers

Young adults, ages twelve through eighteen

Setting

The New York Public Library includes, besides four research libraries, eighty-two branch libraries whose mission it is to meet the educational, informational, and cultural needs of millions of New Yorkers of every age and ethnic background. The Office of Young Adult Services has provided programs and materials to meet the special needs and interests of teenagers since 1919. The Chatham Square Regional Library Branch is in Manhattan's Chinatown.

Program Description

The Young Adult Mural Project took place in the Chatham Square Branch Library from late June to early September 1993. The purpose of the project was to provide a group of young adults with the opportunity to plan, design, and create a large-scale painting that ultimately would be placed on permanent display in the main reading room of the branch. The idea for this project came from a desire to provide a group of young people from the Chinatown community with an opportunity to spend the summer in a unique and exciting way; to establish a regular, weekly activity; and to make a very visible contribution to the library and the community. By working on such a project, young participants would learn some very useful skills, such as working

Permanent dragon mural depicting cultural heritage of Chatham branch library.

together and patience in planning, and gain a tremendous sense of gratification once the mural was completed. It was felt that such a project would help beautify the library and also help to strengthen the bonds between the library and the community as a whole.

Work on the project began when an artist was recruited to lead the project, almost two months before the initial group session. A decision was made to meet every Monday for two hours from June to early September, with a gala unveiling ceremony sometime around the opening of the school year. To recruit young adults, flyers and project descriptions were sent to community agencies, schools, and local papers; and postings were made in the branch. Young people were approached personally by staff members and given information during class visits and programs held by the young-adult librarian. Forty YAs began the project, but the group settled down to a core of about twenty. This core came enthusiastically without fail to each session, working with the artist, the YA librarian, and a community advisor to plan, design, draw, and paint. The excitement generated by the project managed to spread to every imaginable corner of the branch library as well as throughout the community.

Finally, on September ninth, the unveiling celebration was held, with community leaders, teachers, representatives from the Office of Young Adult Services, librarians from other branches, a local reporter, and just about every young adult who had contributed to the mural and their friends in attendance. When the cover cloth was removed, the beautiful design was seen—a glittering dragon whose body was covered with community scenes was poised in flight, through a swirling blue sky and up a gleaming red staircase toward what could be thought of as a destination of Wisdom and Harmony. The group gasped and shrieked with joy and satisfaction. Camera bulbs flashed jubilantly. During the ceremony that followed, a slide show of the project was presented, speeches were made, flowers and thank you cards were exchanged, and every participant was given a special certificate by the library.

Community in Motion, the title of the mural, was deemed a success, which can be understood quite well through the comments and faces of the many library users who pass it or sit beneath it as it hangs majestically in the Chatham Square Regional Branch Library.

Funding

The entire cost of $720 was underwritten from the budget of the Office of Young Adult Services ($600 for the artist for eight sessions at $75 each and $120 for supplies).

Contact Person

Jeff Katz, Young Adult Librarian, Chatham Square Regional Branch, New York Public Library, 33 East Broadway, New York, NY 10002. (212) 964-6598

Index

Mary K. Chelton, a co-founder of *Voice of Youth Advocates,* has been a youth services advocate for over twenty years. She has held positions in five public library systems and numerous offices within ALA and state associations. She was a consultant to both first and second national surveys on young adult services in public libraries from the U.S. Department of Education, and she is the 1985 winner of ALA's Grolier Foundation Award for outstanding service to young people.